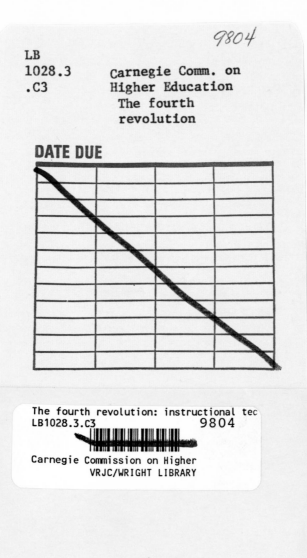

The Fourth Revolution

INSTRUCTIONAL TECHNOLOGY IN HIGHER EDUCATION

A Report and Recommendations by

The Carnegie Commission on Higher Education

JUNE 1972

The Fourth Revolution

INSTRUCTIONAL TECHNOLOGY IN HIGHER EDUCATION

A Report and Recommendations by
The Carnegie Commission on Higher Education
JUNE 1972

MCGRAW-HILL BOOK COMPANY
New York   St. Louis   San Francisco   Düsseldorf
London   Sydney   Toronto   Mexico   Panama
Johannesburg   Kuala Lumpur   Montreal
New Delhi   Rio de Janeiro   Singapore

*This report is issued by the Carnegie Commission on
Higher Education, with headquarters at
1947 Center Street, Berkeley, California 94704.
The views and conclusions expressed in this report
are solely those of the members of the Carnegie Commission
on Higher Education and do not necessarily reflect the
views or opinions of the Carnegie Corporation of New York,
The Carnegie Foundation for the Advancement of Teaching,
or their trustees, officers, directors, or employees.*

Library of Congress Cataloging in Publication Data

Carnegie Commission on Higher Education.
The fourth revolution.
Bibliography: p.
1. Education technology. I. Title.
LB1028.3.C3   378.1'7   72-4363
ISBN 0-07-010050-0

*Additional copies of this report may be ordered from
McGraw-Hill Book Company, Hightstown, New Jersey 08520.
The price is $1.95 a copy.*

Any technology which increases the rate of learning would enable (as Comenius put it centuries ago) the teacher to teach less and the learner to learn more.

SIR ERIC ASHBY

Contents

Foreword

The technology of communications and data processing that has had such a profound impact on American society generally in recent decades promises to have powerful influences on higher education as well. What these influences may be and what steps should be taken to assure that the benefits of instructional technology will be realized in an orderly and reasonably prompt manner are the concerns of this report.

On the following pages we acknowledge the utilization of technology for administrative and research tasks in higher learning, but emphasize its role in *instruction.* Moreover, for purposes of this report, a distinction is made between *instruction* that is designed for a formal teaching-learning situation, and the more general *information* that may result from informal exposure to information and ideas. For example, recent studies on public broadcast television and community antenna television were concerned with general policies involved in the regulation and use of these media.[1] Both studies gave considerable attention to the educational capabilities of television, but both studies also deferred questions concerning instructional uses of the media by institutions as subjects for closer consideration by those specifically concerned with educational endeavors. By the same token, in this report we are only incidentally concerned with the informal educational potentials of television, while we are very much concerned with the uses of television for instruction.

In assessing impacts of technology on the campuses, we expect students to benefit from it because it offers them greater flexibility and more alternatives in their learning experience. Faculty mem-

---

[1] See Carnegie Commission on Educational Television (1967) and The Sloan Commission on Cable Communications (1971).

bers, we find, now tend to be resistant or apathetic in their attitudes toward instructional technology. But there are signs that they, too, have much to gain if the new media are introduced to colleges and universities in appropriate ways.

Particular emphasis is given to the direction of new effort that is required if the full advantages of technology in higher education are to be realized.

Many persons have been consulted and have given us helpful suggestions for this report. We have also benefited greatly from the writings and reports of other organizations. Our findings and recommendations are mostly a blend of suggestions and practice which, on the basis of our experience and careful evaluation, we consider to have the greatest merit as part of a coherent policy.

We wish particularly to acknowledge our indebtedness to the Commission on Instructional Technology, which, under the chairmanship of Sterling McMurrin, has produced, with the editorship of Dr. Sidney Tickton, the most comprehensive documentation on current instructional technology presently available in a single report. The existence of this report makes extensive analysis of specific instructional and media programs unnecessary in our own document. We also would like to express particular appreciation to Roger E. Levien of the RAND Corporation who directed a thorough and invaluable study of computer-assisted instruction for the Commission and has consulted with us on certain portions of this report. His study, entitled *The Emerging Technology*, will be published by McGraw-Hill in 1972 as part of the Carnegie Commission on Higher Education series. We also have drawn upon "Will Information Technologies Help Learning?," an essay by Anthony G. Oettinger with Nikki Zapol, which will be published later this year in a Commission volume edited by Carl Kaysen on the undergraduate curriculum.

We wish also to thank members of our staff, particularly Verne A. Stadtman, for their work in preparing this report, and to express our appreciation to Robert D. Tschirgi and Richard B. Curtis who contributed to earlier considerations of this topic.

Eric Ashby
The Master
Clare College
Cambridge, England

Ralph M. Besse
Chairman of the Board
National Machinery Company

The Fourth Revolution

1. Major Themes and Marginal Observations

1 Higher education (and education generally) now faces the first great technological revolution in five centuries in the potential impact of the new electronics.

2 New technology has already transformed *(a)* research techniques in many fields and *(b)* administrative methods on many campuses. It is now *(c)* affecting large libraries and *(d)* is entering into the instructional process. Our estimates of the current status and potential utilization of information technology in higher education are shown in Figure 1. The new technology may provide the single greatest opportunity for academic change on and off campus.

3 The experience thus far with the new technology (applied to instruction), however, as compared with the hopes of its early supporters, indicates that it is *(a)* coming along more slowly, *(b)* costing more money, and *(c)* adding to rather than replacing older approaches — as the teacher once added to what the family could offer, as writing then added to oral instruction, as the book later added to the handwritten manuscript.

4 Nevertheless, by the year 2000 it now appears that a significant proportion of instruction in higher education on campus may be carried on through informational technology — perhaps in a range of 10 to 20 percent. It certainly will penetrate much further than this into off-campus instruction at levels beyond the secondary school — in fact it may become dominant there at a level of 80 percent or more.

Better than ever before, it can bring education to the sick, the handicapped, the aged, the prisoners, the members of the armed forces, persons in remote areas, and to many adults who could at-

FIGURE 1 *Estimated use of electronic technology (computers, "cable" television, videocassettes) in higher education*

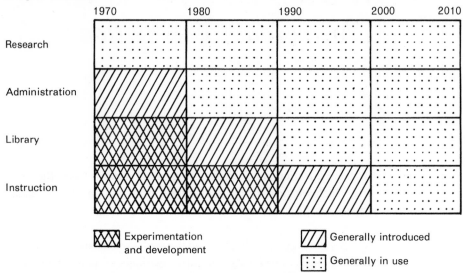

SOURCE: Staff of the Carnegie Commission on Higher Education.

tend classes on campus but who will find instruction at home more convenient. It can create new uses for leisure time, can facilitate job-to-job movement through new training, and can improve community participation by imparting greater skill and knowledge to citizens. Informational technology is already heavily used in the armed forces and in in-plant training in industry. It is more widely used now in primary and secondary schools than in on-campus higher education and will continue to be used more at those levels in the future. The new technology will also tend to draw instruction from the historical requirements-met-through-teaching approach to a resources-available-for-learning approach; and this can be a fundamental change.

5   For students, the expanding technology has two major advantages: properly applied, it increases the opportunities for independent study, and it provides students with a richer variety of courses and methods of instruction. Students can choose, for example, between a lecture and a computer program, thus introducing competition between the two techniques and potentially raising the quality of instruction in both. Or they can choose total immersion in one subject at a time. They have more options. Much of the new tech-

nology, additionally, is infinitely tolerant and infinitely patient toward the slow learner. It also does not act *in loco parentis* toward anybody. We will note in a forthcoming report *(Reform on Campus)* that two complaints of students are the inadequate variety of courses available to them and the lack of quality in some classroom instruction. The expanding technology can speak to both of these complaints. It can also help supply answers to the two great aspects of "humanization" of higher education (1) by making access easier and (2) by paying more attention to the specific needs of individual students. Students, in order to make good use of the new instructional methods at the college level, must be given new learning skills beginning at least in high school.

For faculty members, the new technology can lessen routine instructional responsibilities in the more elementary work in languages, mathematics, the sciences, accounting, and other fields. It may, however, reduce the need for both teaching assistants and for additional new faculty members at a time when requirements for them are lessening for other reasons. We do not expect, however, that it will lead to the replacement of any present faculty members. It does mean that faculty members of the future will need more training in the new instructional techniques. We believe that the Doctor of Arts degree we have recommended earlier is particularly adapted to the new situation. Faculty members will, of necessity, need to adjust to the new division of labor. Historically they have been all-around journeymen with helpers (TAs), and now they will be working with technicians as well. The academic manning table becomes more complex as it has already become in so many other fields, as for example, in the health professions. Within campus-bound higher education, the techniques of informational technology may well influence instructional methods by making them more carefully thought out even if none of the new technology is used in a particular course. Most or even all instruction will become more analytical in its approach, more conscious about its methods.

For financing authorities, the new informational technology will eventually reduce instructional costs below levels possible using conventional methods alone, but, in the short run, it will only increase costs. It will be financially prudent to concentrate early investments in areas with the greatest capability for wide use: *(a)* libraries, *(b)* adult education, *(c)* primary and secondary education, and *(d)* introductory courses in higher education where basic skills are involved, like mathematics and language.

6 Some implications of the new informational technology are:

- Off-campus instruction of adults may become both the most rapidly expanding and the most rapidly changing segment of postsecondary education.

- Fewer students may study on campus, and more may elect to pursue their studies off campus and get credit by examination. This will reduce enrollments below the levels they otherwise would reach.

- Students in small colleges will have more access to a greater variety of courses and greater library resources. The big campus will have fewer advantages on these scores.

- The library, if it becomes the center for the storage and retrieval of knowledge in whatever form, will become a more dominant feature of the campus. New libraries should be planned with the potential impact of technology in mind.

- New buildings should be built with adequate electronic components. They should also be planned for 24-hour use.

- Some new colleges and universities may be constructed with a central core area and with satellite campuses scattered around within commuting distance. The core area will provide access to knowledge; the satellite campuses will provide a greater sense of community because of their smaller size.

- New configurations will take place to the extent that students are dispersed as consumers and as some faculty members and many technicians are concentrated as producers.

- New professions of multimedia technologists are being born.

- Students will need to be more familiar with the use of certain technologies — particularly the computer — as they begin their college training.

- Prospective high school teachers and prospective college and university teachers will need to be trained in the use of the new technologies for instruction. Many of these prospective teachers who are in college now will still be teaching in the year 2000 when the new technology will be in general use in educational institutions.

- Universities and colleges will be able to trade-off in their overall budget making between funds for construction of buildings for on-campus instruction and operating costs of off-campus instruction.

- Less remedial instruction will be necessary on campus. Students will come to college better prepared or will receive their remedial instruction in off-campus courses or through independent learning assisted by the new technology.

- Good systems for informing and advising students will become more essential and more complex as additional options are made available and as more instructional opportunities are located off campus.

- Many more and better tests will be required to evaluate the progress of students who learn through the new forms of instructional technology.

- Some of the informational technology, thus far, seems better at training skills than at general education. The better it is at training skills, the more general education may suffer as a result—particularly if students move off campus and content themselves with skill training. But instructional technology, represented by such media as television and film, can also contribute to general education and to the teaching of concepts.

- Some equivalent of the university press, or an expanded university press, may eventually be necessary to produce videocassettes and other instructional software that can be used with the new technology.

- Copyright laws will need to be reviewed by Congress to adapt them to the new carriers of information.

7   The new technology will have a centralizing effect:

(a) On campus there will need to be some agency (whether it is the library or some other facility) that will provide equipment and materials, assist in the preparation of programs, and aid in the presentation of programs.

(b) Among campuses, there will be a need for cooperation on a regional or even national basis. We propose the establishment of at least seven regionally organized cooperative learning-technology centers not only for research and development activities, but also for production and distribution of instructional programs designed for use with the expanded media. Such centers will also serve as badly needed information sources for participating members who need to know what instructional materials are available, and which technologies are best applied to specific instructional problems. Participating institutions should be regarded as members of such centers and should have a voice in their policies. Such centers will need to have a full measure of academic freedom and autonomy, for their programs will be more widely influential than many textbooks; and textbooks, on occasion, have become sensitive subjects. Because we lack experience in the operation of such centers, we recommend that they be created, at least initially, on a staggered basis—one every three years until all are completed.

8 There are important roles for governments, industry, and certain nonprofit organizations to play in providing financial support, developing distribution systems, and designing and perfecting instructional software. We believe that no single segment of society should totally dominate the development of instructional materials in higher education and that colleges and universities should take initiative in such activities along with other instrumentalities.

An alternative approach to development of instructional materials on campus and in regional centers and by industry is to set up instructional programs dependent upon the expanded technologies in a separate, competitive national system (as in Japan). A system of this kind might make rapid progress with considerable economy. We prefer, however, that the new instructional technologies be developed in a somewhat more diversified setting in which faculty members also have an opportunity to exercise strong influence. Instruction developed that way will be more readily accepted in the academic community and will be less subject to political intrusion. We prefer a competitive approach with instrumentalities of higher education involved in the competition.

9 The specific new technologies, among the many available, which hold out the greatest prospects in the longer run are:

- Cable TV
- Videocassettes
- Computer-assisted instruction
- Learning kits to be used with audiovisual independent study units

Industry will have the major responsibility for developing and manufacturing the "hardware." Great attention needs to be paid to making instructional components for these media more compatible among the models of several producers than they now are—as has happened previously with record players and TV sets.

10 The federal government will need to provide not only the bulk of the research and development funds, as it has in the past, but also funds for distribution of effective instructional programs that use the expanded technology. We believe that the new technology warrants a minimal expenditure of about $100 million for well-targeted support in 1973, including funds for cooperative learning-technology centers. We recommend that annual federal expenditures for research, development, and utilization of the new media should increase from the $100 million proposed for 1973 until they reach a sum equal to 1 percent of total national expenditures on higher education. We consider this a wise long-term investment.

11 Higher education should cautiously welcome the new informational technology, not resist it. We see no need for academic Luddites. But, on the other hand, "program or perish" should not replace "publish or perish."

12 Constant evaluation of the results among alternative approaches and of total costs and total consequences will be essential. For example, students learn from each other: Does the new technology reduce this interchange? And faculty members serve as models to their students: To what extent may this contribution be lost? Some independent assessment projects or agencies should be established in the very near future to provide ongoing and impartial study of the total impacts of the new technology.

13 The proposed National Institute of Education can be very helpful with research and development, and the proposed National Foundation for Postsecondary Education can be helpful with innovative programs at the campus level.

14 The United States with its great resources may be able to develop programs and techniques which can extend the advantages of greater learning to less wealthy nations of the world, aiding them to raise their literacy and skill levels faster and at less cost — but any element of political indoctrination must be totally absent. The whole world can be assisted to move faster into becoming a "Learning Society."

2. The Fourth Revolution

Eric Ashby (1967) has identified four revolutions in education.

- The first revolution occurred when societies began to differentiate adult roles, and the task of educating the young was shifted, in part, from parents to teachers and from the home to the school.
- The second, which in some places antedated the first, "was the adoption of the written word as a tool of education." Prior to that time, oral instruction prevailed, and it was only with reluctance that writing was permitted to coexist with the spoken word in the classroom.
- The third revolution came with the invention of printing and the subsequent wide availability of books.
- The fourth revolution, in Ashby's view, is portended by developments in electronics, notably those involving the radio, television, tape recorder, and computer.

The fourth revolution has been emerging from the realm of prophecy for at least three decades. The electronic media that give it its most futuristic characteristics already exist. So do certain problems to which the new media appear to offer acceptable, and sometimes spectacular, solutions. The most obvious of these problems is the ever-expanding dimension of higher education—the opening of educational opportunity to greater numbers of students; the lengthening list of subjects to be taught; the growing variety of student interests and objectives to be served; the increasing societal demands to be satisfied; and the incessant enlargement of the intellectual domain. Mere replication of existing traditional institutions is not an adequate response to growth of this magnitude. Something else is needed, and the new technology is at least part of it.

In the 1960s, when a shortage of professors for our colleges and universities was anticipated, instructional technology was viewed as a means of making learning more independent of instructors and of spreading faculty time over more students. It was soon discovered that independent learning did not save time or yield spectacular economies in all cases, but it proved advantageous for other reasons. It gave students an opportunity to play a more active role in their own learning. It provided alternative modes of instruction for students who did not learn well in conventional classes. It provided ways for students to undertake learning at different rates of speed, without either holding back or pushing the pace of an entire class.

Independent learning also has logistical advantages—such as allowing students greater flexibility in the scheduling of classes, permitting repetition of presentations missed because of illness, and, in some cases, allowing the instruction to take place in the student's room or in a carrel in the library or residence hall. At the adult level, it can take education to a student's place of employment or to his living room. It can also penetrate hospitals and prisons.

The work of faculty members and technologists to devise instructional materials that use the new media effectively has aroused new interest in learning theory and its application to the planning of courses, curricular design, and even the arrangement of physical facilities in which learning takes place. Behavioral scientists have joined the fourth revolution and have served usefully in pointing out the importance of defining learning objectives and suggesting ways in which natural learning processes can be utilized in the presentation of subject matter. Part of their contribution has been to take the machinery of the fourth revolution out of the spotlight and to assign such novel media as computers and television a place in the ranks alongside the slide projector, the textbook, and the teacher as useful participants. This integration of new media, long-familiar technology, planning of instructional space, learning theory, and the professor into a total effort is sometimes called the "systems approach" or the "learning environment approach" to instruction. This view now has international acceptance. In 1971, in a preface to a report based on an international workshop, J. R. Gass of the Organization for Economic Cooperation and Development wrote: "Educational technology is not a bag of mechanical tricks, but the organized design and implementation of learning systems, taking advantage of, but not expecting miracles from, modern communications methods, visual aids, classroom organization and teaching methods" (Centre for Education Research and Innovation [CERI], 1971, p. 7).[1]

WHEN SHOULD TECHNOLOGY BE USED? We believe that technology should be the servant and not the master of instruction. It should not be adopted merely because it exists, or because an institution fears that it will be left behind the parade of progress without it.

We also believe that sophisticated technology is not to be equated with saturation. In some courses, the use of technology may be appropriate only for a few hours in an entire term. In a few, technology may be constructively used for two-thirds of the hours allotted for a term of instruction; in a very few, it may take over the entire process.

The following two tests should be applied in deciding whether any technology (including conventional modes) is to be used or not:[2]

- The teaching-learning task to be performed should be essential to the course of instruction to which it is applied.

- The task to be performed could not be performed as well—if at all—for the students served without the technology contemplated.

Institutions that apply these tests faithfully will at once generate confidence in the technology that is used and preserve the humanistic qualities of the educational process.

---

[1] Two years earlier the U.S. Department of Health, Education and Welfare's Commission on Instructional Technology (The McMurrin Commission) offered a definition with slightly more emphasis on the role of learning theory. It defines educational technology as ". . . a systematic way of designing, carrying out, and evaluating the total process of learning and teaching in terms of specific objectives, based on research in human learning and communications, and employing a combination of human resources to bring about more effective instruction" (Tickton, 1970, 1, p. 22).

[2] These two principles are adapted from a paper submitted to the Commission on Instructional Technology by The Research and Development Office of the National Association of Education Broadcasters. That document referred to "two discriminating tests: (1) the teaching-learning task involved must be intensively valuable, even critical, to contemporary educational operations; (2) the task could not be performed as well—if at all—without television mediation."

THE NEED FOR SOFTWARE The fourth revolution will not mature in a fortnight. In fact, it now seems to be faltering.

The principal deficiency is in the availability of computer programs, video- and audiotapes, printed learning modules, films and other "software" of instructional technology. This deficiency exists for six important reasons.

1 Instructional technology is not uniformly welcomed by the academic community.

2 Faculty members who are interested in designing learning materials for the new instructional technology usually are not properly rewarded for their efforts.

3 Although the physical equipment of instructional technology exists, there is little compatibility of components in models of some mediaware made by different manufacturers. This incompatibility forces nontechnologists to guess which models are most likely to dominate the educational market before proceeding with the design of learning materials.

4 There is ongoing debate over the relative virtues of learning materials produced for local campus use and those produced for national distribution. We believe that a combination effort will be most fruitful. On the campuses, faculty members should be encouraged to develop new instructional programs with the assistance of educational technicians and media specialists. Beyond the campuses, teams in consortia of institutions, in learned and professional societies, and in the communications and information industries should be similarly engaged. The quality of the programs thus developed will vary widely for the next decade or so, but as more programs become available it will be increasingly possible for faculty members to be selective on a qualitative basis. If a program fully satisfies the instructional objectives of a course or course segment, it will be a valid choice for classroom use regardless of its point of origin.

5 Few faculty members have the combined interests and expertise in subject matter, media development, and learning theory that the design of high-quality instructional materials requires. Some campuses do not have this combination of expertise available even in different individuals.

6 Faculty members have been disenchanted by persistent findings in many studies[3] that the learning effectiveness of instruction provided by technology is not significantly different from that of "good professors and teachers using conventional modes of instruction." As Anthony Oettinger (1972, forthcoming) points out, these findings tend to "fly in the face of common sense," and ". . . confirm limitations of formal research on schooling rather than deny the impact of technology on learning" (ibid., p. 5). Such findings overlook advantages of technological applications that may not be measured in current research. In interpretations of the findings, sufficient care is not always taken to make clear that while "no difference" does not necessarily mean "better," it also does not necessarily mean "worse." The studies that produced these findings have been of great value and have properly restrained unbridled enthusiasm, but they should not prevent educators and manufacturers from efforts to design and use effective learning materials.

Although we believe colleges and universities should assume greater initiative in the development and use of instructional technology generally, we do not entirely regret that they are moving cautiously. Overdevelopment of technology for relatively limited objectives could complicate the ultimate integration of technology into well-developed teaching and learning systems. Moreover, considerable amounts of the "new" technology turn out, on investigation, to be reinventions of simpler technologies already in use. Finally, the mere possession of learning media cannot guarantee an educational advantage for an institution. To be effective, technology must be used by inspired and skillful teachers and staff members who will not abandon it when they and their students lose enthusiasm for the novelty of the media adopted. Instructional media must also be stored, maintained, and eventually replaced when they wear out or become obsolete. Institutions that plan to

---

[3] The most comprehensive review of such studies that relate to instructional use of television has been done by Chu and Schramm (1967). The two authors reviewed, up to 1966, 207 published studies in which television teaching was compared with conventional teaching. Of the 421 separate comparisons made in these studies, 308 showed no significant differences, 63 showed television instruction to be superior, and 50 found conventional instruction better (ibid., p. 100). They also found, however, that instructional television can more easily be used effectively for primary and secondary school students than for college students. Findings in a similar vein have been reported for instructional use of computers, films, and programmed instruction (e.g., Levien, 1972, in press).

utilize more instructional technology should, therefore, be prepared to incur the expenses required by such activities.

But the overriding reason for caution is that it is in the nature of revolutions that their impact is greater than the changes immediately perceived. The social and political consequences of completion of the transcontinental railroad is one example. The way books and television are now taken for granted in most homes and influence our lives in many subtle ways is another example closer to the point. The expanding technology in higher education, in the same way, is certain to have implications for colleges and universities that transcend its immediate role in the classrooms.

3. A Brief Review of Instructional Technology

Many examples of educational technology are so familiar that they are taken for granted. Books, after all, are technological aids to learning. Another is the blackboard, which is virtually the universal symbol of the classroom. The charts, maps, models, and specimens displayed in classroom demonstrations today are but improved and modernized versions of materials customarily found in the "cabinets" of science professors of the mid-nineteenth century. The stereograph was familiar in the classroom by 1885; its direct-line descendant, the lantern slide, was widely used in the early 1900s. Motion pictures were introduced into the classroom in 1910 and radio in the 1920s (Saettler, 1968).

THE PRINTED WORD

Familiar technologies are sometimes combined with others or used in new ways for maximum impact, and the book is a dramatic example. Microfilm and microfiche can shrink large volumes into relatively small packages or even to a 4- by 6-inch card. Mechanical readers enlarge the reduced copies to readable size again. Still another family of technology oriented to books includes the reading pacers and other devices designed to teach people to read faster. Dry-copying processes eliminate copious notetaking from printed materials and facilitate the sharing of excerpts. Printed matter can be electronically reproduced, virtually on command, for reception miles away from a transmitter. All this technology exists now, and some of it is no longer regarded with much amazement by the average college student.

FILM

Although motion pictures have been available to educators for more than 60 years, they have been used somewhat sporadically for instruction. Seeking out and then acquiring suitable films for use has often been an annoying chore. Good films often have been relatively expensive and, in order to use them, faculty members have frequently had to move their students to a theater or some other properly equipped hall. Sometimes, they also have had to hire the services of a projectionist. Some of these drawbacks have been eliminated with the expanding use of 8-mm film, which is inexpensive, easy to store, and often packaged in cassettes that can be loaded into small projectors and operated by an individual student at his or her own convenience. It is becoming a preferred medium for presenting visual materials emphasizing movement in very brief segments as short as two or four minutes. In its 8-mm brief presentation form, it is a familiar component of some of the self-instruction laboratories that are described subsequently in this section.

MULTIMEDIA CLASSROOMS
There is nothing very new about the idea of including short motion pictures, slides, live demonstrations, musical segments, or portions of taped interviews in a lecture presentation. But, until recently, the major accommodation of technology in the presentation of such material has been to include a projection booth in the back of major lecture rooms. Some colleges and universities now provide more sophisticated arrangements. For example, in 1965, a new instructional building called the Forum was completed at Pennsylvania State University. It consists of four lecture halls, each accommodating 396 students. A central core contains equipment for projecting slides, 16-mm films and television on screens in each of the halls. Each screen can accommodate two images side by side or one central image. Facilities also exist for audiotape recording and playback. A small television camera in each auditorium can be used to magnify small objects and demonstrations for projection on the large screen. All the projection equipment in the central core may be operated by the instructor from his lectern or may be controlled by a technician in the central core (Thorton & Brown, 1968).

In certain classrooms of other institutions, students may take advantage of an electronic response system that enables them to transmit their answers to multiple-choice questions inserted at frequent intervals within the lecture content. Their feedback is immediately available to the instructor and shows him when it is time to move on to a new topic, or to review material that has not yet been adequately comprehended. It also gives students "test-as-you-go" measurement of their own progress in relation to the pace of the class as a whole.

Multimedia classrooms are found on several American campuses today, particularly in buildings erected within the past 25 years.

SELF-INSTRUCTION UNITS Some of the same media employed in multimedia classrooms, where large numbers of students are taught simultaneously — and somewhat passively — are employed in self-instruction units.

Language Laboratories A specialized variant of the self-instruction unit is the language laboratory. Typically, such a facility consists of booths for 24 to 60 students. Each booth is equipped with a tape recorder capable of duplicating, playback, listen-record, and audiolingual testing. The teacher operates a console which can record student responses, monitor student responses, test, correct student responses, and give instructions either to individual students or to all students simultaneously (Allen & Coombs, 1970).

Audiolistening Centers The basic component of most of the newly introduced "mechanized" individualized learning centers is the tape recorder. It has the virtues of easy operation and maintenance and an adaptability to a wide range of instructional uses. It has been used most intensively in language instruction, speech, drama, and education, where students need opportunities to hear their own voices. Like the language laboratory, the audiolistening unit usually takes the form of a carrel. Tape-playback equipment is basic, but other media, such as short 8-mm film and slides, can be introduced relatively easily.

Individual Learning Laboratories A considerably more advanced version of the independent learning unit is the individual learning laboratory. Originally it was designed to help freshmen in a botany course at Purdue to master basic information essential to an understanding of the course. Eventually, tape-recorded sessions replaced the lectures. Learning units were carefully planned by the professor involved, coordinating what the student heard on tape with what he read in his textbook. By a process of evolution, these laboratories now provide an instructional experience that combines listening to explanations and instructions on tape; reading assignments in textbooks; use of films, slides, and other visuals; as well as student-conducted experiments guided by instruction sheets and tapes. In courses where they are used (and they seem to be used most widely in biological sciences at the present time), they normally replace two lectures delivered under traditional weekly instruction plans. We are aware of particularly successful use of such units at Simon Frazer University and San Jose State College in California.

Remote-access Units

Still another refinement of the individual instruction unit is the use of computing equipment and telephone lines to control and deliver access to audio and visual instructional materials maintained in a central storage center. The effect is to give students access to audio and visual instructional materials virtually at command, from a carrel in the library or some other building on the campus, or even from their own rooms. There is no technical reason why reception must be confined to a carrel when, with appropriate communication links, it can be obtained at one's place of work, or one's own living room almost as easily.

INSTRUC-TIONAL USE OF THE RADIO

Broadcast instruction has been with us since the 1920s, but efforts to develop educational radio stations eventually seemed to founder on inadequate financing, insurmountable competition with the popular offerings on commercial radio and television, unimaginative use of the medium, and apathy both within the radio industry and the educational establishment. By 1967–68, the Ohio State University's radio station, which had helped to launch the use of radio in schools, was broadcasting only two programs a week to schools (Tickton, 1970, p. 69). By 1970, only 25 educational AM radio stations out of 202 that had been licensed by the Federal Communications Commission remained in existence. One of these was Portland's KBPS, which developed over 100 series for school use and served Portland's public schools for 45 years (Breitenfeld, 1970, p. 157). The number of FM stations has continued to grow since the first one was licensed in 1938. In 1970, 457 were in existence and two-thirds of these went on the air after 1970. Most of them are operated by educational institutions and have a broadcast radius of only two to five miles. Only 10 to 15 percent of the stations are primarily instructional, however, in the sense that they broadcast directly to classrooms (Forsythe, 1970, pp. 2, 3). Radio has been used extensively in Sweden, South Korea, Japan, and Great Britain for instructional purposes and has obvious advantages for delivering education to remote areas. In schools and colleges in the United States, it is frequently used in combination with other technologies — slides, or even television. One of the most fascinating uses in American higher education is exemplified by a program at Albany Medical College wherein receivers and transmitters are installed in 71 participating hospitals. Doctors assemble around the receivers to hear presentations by the Albany Medical College faculty. Slides, charts, and x-rays are made available to the listening groups, and doctors in attendance can ask questions that are heard throughout the network. This operation, using facilities of station WAMC, is described as "the largest postgraduate classroom in the world." Similar networks are found in North Carolina, California, Utah, and Ohio (Forsythe, 1970, p. 3).

INSTRUC-TIONAL TELEVISION Televised instruction comes in many forms, and each has slightly different capacities and limitations.

Broadcast Television This is the type of television communication most Americans understand best. Its distinguishing characteristic is transmission of television signals over the air. Channels are allotted to both commercial and noncommercial broadcasters. Open broadcast programs can be received by anyone with an antenna, but only one signal (or program) can be transmitted by a broadcasting station at a time.

Both commercial and noncommercial stations and networks have made efforts in the past to provide programming considered to be of educational value. Noncommercial stations especially have been engaged in such endeavors. As we note elsewhere in this report, BBC's "Civilisation" and CBS's "Interview With Lord North," widely viewed over American stations, have been adapted for instructional use on at least one American campus. Such series as "Masterpiece Theatre" and "The Advocates" have attracted wide audiences within the general public and are highly regarded for their educational value. "Sesame Street" and "Electric Company," created as programs to help build learning skills of young children, have proved spectacularly appealing to their audiences and effective in meeting their objectives. Moreover, they have demonstrated the importance of designing learning experiences that make the most of the advantages the medium of television has to offer.

Some colleges and universities have been able to use broadcast facilities for instructional purposes. One of the oldest and most successful instructional programs on broadcast television is Chicago's TV College, broadcast as an extension of Chicago City College. It is now in its eleventh year. The college is on the air about 25 hours a week, presenting nine courses on a credit or noncredit basis. Approximately 350 students have completed requirements for an associate in arts certificate offered on completion of the program. Another 2,150 graduates have completed about one semester's work on television. The college enrolls chronically ill and handicapped students, and students who are confined to penal institutions. The TV College also broadcasts television courses to students on the Chicago City College campus when departments request it to do so. Open broadcast television is the medium, for the present, for about 10 percent of the instruction offered by Great Britain's Open University.

Closed-circuit Television

This is the most frequently encountered instructional use of television. It uses cables ("wires") to transmit signals from one point to another. On college campuses, television wiring is often laid from building to building, forming a closed campus network. Its capabilities are:

- Increasing the range of instruction to one or more locations beyond the classroom of origin

- Magnifying exhibits and demonstrations difficult to see in a normal classroom situation (for which it is used extensively in schools of medicine and dentistry)

- Presenting live situations that would be difficult or impossible to view unobtrusively under other circumstances (live classroom instruction, therapy for the mentally ill)

- Exchanging professors and courses between one institution and another linked to a circuit

- Enabling colleges to present televised instruction in accordance with their own schedules and needs

Particularly advantageous is the ability to transmit more than one signal through the same interconnecting cable at the same time.

Instructional Television Fixed Service

This method of signal distribution is characterized by broadcast signals at very high frequencies that can be picked up only with special receiving equipment. The range of coverage is from 8 to 25 miles—more than adequate for many colleges and universities.

Cable Television

The extended counterpart of the campuswide closed-circuit television system is Community Antenna Television. In this system, specially designed antennas on high towers or mountain tops pick up television signals from distant points, strengthen them, and then distribute them to homes, businesses, and schools over special cables. In public use of cable systems, service is obtained for a monthly fee, usually between $3 and $6 for each connection. In June 1970 the character and potentials of cable television fell under the close scrutiny of a special commission created by the Alfred P. Sloan Foundation. Its findings have been impressive. For example, the Sloan Commission estimates that by 1980 "the majority of cable franchises will have a capacity of at least twenty channels, that forty-channel systems will be commonplace, or at least well within the state of the art, and that even greater capacity may be found in great metropolitan areas." Also by 1980, the Commission believes that between 40 and 60 percent of the nation's homes will have cable television services (The Sloan Commission, 1971, pp. 37–39).[1]

The most exciting implications of television for education are found in the large number of channels that it makes available. Instead of carrying only one program at a time, the cable can carry many—some of interest to large numbers of people, some of interest to a select few. Put another way: Cable television makes it figuratively unnecessary for the educator to compete with the rock band for a chance to be heard in the main auditorium. He can reach his audience by simply delivering his instruction in another room in the same hall. Instead of having to concentrate instruction on a single course for presentation every day for a week early in the morning, as is often true in broadcast television, an instructor can present his course on cable television at convenient times of the day over longer periods of time. But this, as we shall see subsequently, is only the beginning of cable television's promise.

Videotape Storage of instruction for repetitive use is easily accomplished now with the use of videotapes. They may be played back through monitors in a studio or classroom, stored in a library and checked out for viewing on a suitably equipped monitor in a residence or other listening facility, or replayed through a dial-access system such as the one at Oral Roberts University in Oklahoma. Some institutions make use of videotapes to record the classroom performance of student teachers, musicians, or speech students for instant playback. It is videotape's ability to provide virtually in-

[1] This figure is deemed too high by some experts who hold that this penetration may not be reached before 1985.

stantaneous reproduction that gives it a major advantage over film. Some users also report considerable cost savings in using videotape instead of film.

Videocassettes   Many instructional technologists are eagerly awaiting the general availability of videocassettes. Japan, Germany, and the United States already have models on the market. The user simply attaches the cassette player to his own television set, inserts a cassette, and depresses a button. Videocassettes are also considered sturdier than film, and some of them offer better color and picture quality than widely used film processes. Japanese-model cassettes are about the size of a paperback book. The most obvious instructional advantage of the cassette is that it is highly portable and can be used and reused at will. Before 1985, some technologists expect videodiscs to be available. These can be bound into books —a quality that has obvious implications for combining print and audiovisual materials for instruction. Currently available videotape cassettes have stop, rewind, and playback facility. At the present time, however, videocassette equipment is relatively expensive. The leading Japanese player-recorder costs about U.S. —$1,300. Blank cassettes cost $36 each; recorded cassettes cost $50.

COMPUTER-ASSISTED INSTRUCTION   As a part of a study for the Carnegie Commission on Higher Education directed by Roger E. Levien, George A. Comstock surveyed use of computers for instruction in California. He classified instructional computer use into five categories:

Data processing and computer science   The teaching of computer skills in relative isolation from other disciplines. Here the computer is the principal subject.

Student problem solving and research   Teaching about the computer as a tool for use in some field outside computer science. Here a specific sphere of application is the subject.

Tutorial   Use of the computer as a medium to present instruction directly to the student. Here the computer assists or substitutes for the instructor.

Simulations, demonstrations, and gaming   Use of the computer to simulate, in part, social and physical phenomena. Here, what is simulated is the subject of instruction.

Teacher's aid   Use of the computer to assist the teacher in managing instruction, including recording of grades, attendance, and assignments, as well as the more sophisticated actual guidance of instruction based on student performance. Here the computer enhances instructional efficacy but is not part of the subject confronting the students (Comstock, 1972, p. 225).

Comstock found that the most common area of instructional use is data processing and computer science—reported by 68 of the general institutions in his survey. Teacher's aid and problem solving and research applications were widespread—the former reported by 50 percent of the institutions and the latter by 45 percent. More than a third also report computer use for simulations, demonstrations, and gaming. But only 10 percent of the general institutions report tutorial use. We believe that a major factor in the low utilization of the computer for tutorial use is faculty unawareness of its instructional potentials, followed closely by the lack of sufficient instructional software to encourage widespread usage (ibid.).

For the layman, the world of computing hardware is a labyrinth. Computing units are available in many styles and sizes, are capable of greatly varied information storage and retrieval capacities, and are operable at varying speeds and levels of difficulty. Depending upon the extent of use contemplated and the location of a campus, the educator has options of establishing a campus facility, or utilizing a commercial service or time-sharing academic service off campus to obtain computer capability.

At one end of the range of computing systems being developed for instruction is the University of Illinois' Plato IV. Its designers describe it as a large-scale, computer-controlled teaching system capable of handling 4,000 teaching stations (Bitzer & Skaperdas, 1971, p. 33). At the other end of the range is a proposed system which utilizes "minicomputers" and would allow 100 to 300 user terminals to be served with "very fast response times" and with "flexible algorithmic and data-retrieval service" (Stetten, 1971, p. 35).

Many colleges and universities are now utilizing the time-sharing services of a computing consortium, such as Dartmouth's Regional Consortium with 10 member colleges, the Oregon State Regional Computer Center with 7 member institutions, and the University of Iowa Regional Computer Center with 11 member institutions. Basically, participation in such consortia requires only the installation of terminals and telephone communication lines.

The Computer as Control Often overlooked in discussions of the computer as an instructional tool is its role as the control unit for sophisticated instructional systems. If it were desired, computers could operate fully automated, multimedia classrooms, combining taped lectures, films, audiopresentations, slides, and other materials according to a preset agenda. We have already observed the use of computers as control units for remote-access learning systems that provide random availability of audio- and videotape programs on commands transmitted by a telephone dial.

What, then, might happen if complete volumes of technical journals, or indeed, entire sets of encyclopedias could be miniaturized for storage on videocassettes that could be transmitted at random request by users anywhere—in homes, libraries, or study carrels—for reproduction on a standard television screen with stop-start-backtrack capabilities? The physical equipment and basic know-how for such a system are believed to exist.

The MITRE Corporation has been demonstrating, for some time, the capabilities of a system that combines the technologies of the telephone, cable television, and a computer-controlled information system. To use the system, the student or subscriber dials the company's phone number. The home display unit (a television set) reproduces a directory of services, and the subscriber is instructed to indicate which service he wants by pressing appropriate numbers on his telephone. In demonstrations, the services include 27 fourth-grade arithmetic lessons developed under the supervision of Stanford's Patrick Suppes. Community services available include baseball scores, weather forecasts, classified advertisements, a telephone directory, and weekly TV guide. In March 1972, the National Science Foundation provided $10 million for the experimental instructional adaptation of such a system for two-year colleges.

A Concluding Note about Computers

We believe that computers potentially have an important role to play as instructional devices. In 1970, Dartmouth's Kiewit Center was utilized by 2,423 undergraduates and 478 graduates (Kiewit Computation Center, 1971, p. 7). That was more than half of the institution's total student body, which was about 4,000 that year. But nationwide, despite all the money colleges and universities have invested in computing within the past 30 years, only about 4.5 percent of enrolled students[2] have had instructional experience with the computer. As we have already pointed out, part of the problem is faculty apathy and skepticism, part is cost. But another major problem is the paucity of effective teaching programs designed for the computer. A major effort must be made to overcome that deficiency.

We do not emphasize the instructional potential of the computer to give it precedence over other technologies. On the contrary, we believe it must eventually stand as but one of the growing array of technologies that might be selected for any particular instructional use, but it is now a considerably underdeveloped teaching resource that needs attention.

The computer is also a form of technology that holds great promise for fully integrating other available media for instructional use, and that role cannot be ignored if we are to realize the full power of which higher education instruction should be capable in the coming decades.

SOME SIGNIFICANT DEVELOP-MENTS ABROAD

Technology has figured prominently in the efforts of several countries to extend higher educational opportunities to persons who have been unable to take advantage of them in the past. An important target for such programs consists of that part of the population that in the past has had to forego college or university attendance in order to devote full time to earning a living.

Sweden's Television-Radio University

Sweden has been utilizing radio for education for many years. Forsythe (1970, p. 3) reports that Radio Sweden broadcasts more than 166 hours of instruction a year to over 12,000 participating schools. Of more recent origin are plans developed by the Commit-

---

[2] The Levien report estimates that in 1969 the computer expenditures of higher education were $352 million. Computers were used for instruction by 381,000 students (out of 8.5 million) with expenses of $28.4 million (Levien, 1972, in press).

tee for Television and Radio in Education to organize higher-education-level instructional programs with "the idea of creating justice for the generations that have not previously had as great a possibility of obtaining education" (*Television and Radio in Swedish Education*, n.d., p. 1). Its programs have been aimed at the following:

- Technical-natural science programs
- Programs for adult education
- Programs for educational systems at college level including regional experiments and programs for retraining
- Programs for additional university and college education

Early efforts produced about 100 television programs in alegbra and business administration for universities and colleges, college-level courses for adults in business administration (radio and television) and English (radio), and vocational guidance for college-level students. Plans have been announced for other programs on mechanics of materials, mathematical statistics, social studies, psychology, vocational guidance, anatomy, defense and disaster medicine, and economics. Typical instruction combines use of electronic media, printed materials, and live teachers.

University of of the Air in Japan Work on Japan's University of the Air began with a planning committee created in November 1969. Its basic purpose was "the establishment of a new university which uses radio and television as the main means of instruction" (*University of the Air in Japan*, 1970, p. 1). A basic curriculum in technology, natural science, social science, and humanities has been devised. Students who wish to graduate from the University of the Air must study more than four academic years and take more than 124 credits within a prescribed program. Programs are broadcast by television and radio every day of the week from early morning to late at night. Broadcast instruction is supplemented with "seminars, experiments, and practical works given through both broadcasting and institutional schooling" (ibid., p. 4). Although they are not yet in use, Japan intends to make extensive use of videocassettes in its University of the Air programs in the near future.

Great Britain's Open University Described as "perhaps the most ambitious venture in extramural higher education ever undertaken" (Walsh, 1971, p. 675),[1] the

[1] Copyright © 1971 by the American Association for the Advancement of Science.

Open University offers some 24 courses to part-time students 21 years of age and older. With satisfactory completion of prescribed studies, students at the Open University receive bachelor of arts degrees. Teaching by television and radio are an integral part of all its courses, but students also use carefully prepared texts and have access to local study centers located throughout Britain. Students have heavy written-work assignments and are required to attend a one-week summer-school session at a participating university. In its first year, the Open University enrolled 25,000 students out of 42,000 applicants (ibid., p. 676).

West Germany Leadership in the development of extramural studies on the air in West Germany has been taken by broadcasting companies. *The German Tribune* (March 30, 1972, p. 12) reports that one regional network, *Bayerischer Rundfunk,* has been particularly successful. At its inception in 1967, 14,455 people registered for courses, and by 1969 2,878 of them had passed the examinations required for completion. According to the report in *The German Tribune:*

> Every graduate will have followed 460 television broadcasts during the course of his studies, done 144 written studies at home, taken 27 written examinations and spent 59 days at college.

> The work of the tele-college is divided into the television broadcast itself, independent work based on the accompanying literature and the work done later in groups.

Other broadcasting companies in West Germany are also engaged in extramural instruction and efforts of four broadcasting companies to operate a joint college are considered encouraging.

Canada is now contemplating the establishment of an Open University on the British model. In the United States, the new Empire State College is regarded as an "open" alternative to traditional higher education and, like Great Britain's Open University, relies heavily upon materials especially designed by a development faculty, as well as upon community resources, including museums, various health clinics, and local libraries. It is not yet heavily engaged in the use of electronic media. In the fall of 1972, several American institutions will participate experimentally in a program to test the feasibility of using in this country materials developed for Great Britain's Open University.

4. Libraries and the Information Revolution

If electronic communications have generated a fourth revolution in education, the growing abundance of information is certainly generating a fifth. The director of libraries for MIT is credited with the observation that "the worldwide outpouring of printed words is going up 8 to 10 percent a year, with about 400,000 books, 200,000 periodicals, and 200,000 technical reports published in 1968. He indicated that among academic libraries, Harvard has more than eight million volumes, and that there are nearly 100 other universities in this country with more than a million. Each of these hundred is buying annually more than 5 percent of the titles published since Gutenberg" (Cox, 1971, p. 6). Jack Belzer has written that "The proliferation of published materials, the storage, retrieval, dissemination and communication of recorded knowledge can retard our cultural progress, curtail scientific advancement, and drive us to economic disaster" (1970, p. 126). The concern that is evident in these overviews of the information explosion is echoed by private citizens who, each day, become more bewildered by the rich but often conflicting testimony on virtually every subject that is presented on the printed page, over the air waves, and from the public rostrum.

It is at the confluence of the fourth and fifth revolutions that these movements have their greatest momentum and power. And universities, colleges, and their libraries, which operate precisely at this confluence, sense their impacts acutely. For libraries, the impact comes in several forms:

- More information in printed form to catalog and store
- More information in nonprint forms to assimilate into collections traditionally organized in meticulous observance of the conventions of the book and journal production industries

- More clients to serve as the availability of new information becomes apparent
- More clients to serve as the community or campus gets bigger
- More complexity in the interrelations of concepts and ideas and in the ways different people approach the search for information

Libraries have responded to these impacts by seeking additional space, shrinking the size of their collections through weeding procedures and miniaturization techniques, and by automating their operations and services. Some of them have responded by cooperating with one another in the development of catalogs and the sharing of collections and facilities. In the process of these adjustments, some libraries have, themselves, made innovative use of the new electronic media.

MINIATUR- IZATION One of the most advanced undertakings in libraries using modern technology involves the reduction of "hard copy" printed matter to microfilm or microfiche for convenient storage and shipping. Copies of books of up to 100 pages or more are often obtainable from libraries or information centers for $3.00 and up in hard copy editions, but for only 65 cents in microfiche editions that may be no larger than a 4- by 6-inch card. The development of inexpensive "lap readers" could eventually make microfiche as convenient to the user as books. Some technical publications now sell microfiche subscriptions to their products—with unlimited reproduction rights as part of the subscription rate. This costs libraries more for the first copy of publication originally, but can save an institution money on large numbers of duplicate subscriptions on campus. It also enables students and faculty members to reproduce pages and passages relevant to their research—without taking notes—at a relatively low cost.

Librarians who responded to a recent survey expect that "More than 50% of library's new periodicals will be stored on microfilm, microfiche, etc." by 1989. They expect that "More than 50% of library's new books will be stored on microfilm, microfiche, etc." by 2019, and "Library users will receive copies (microfiche or xerox) for a charge of less than 50% of the 1971 price for original materials" by 1989 (Wilcox, 1972, p. 36).

In 1968–69 colleges and universities in the United States reported that miniaturized holdings consisted of 6.3 million reels of microfilm and 58.3 million units of other forms of microtext. This compares to 328.6 million volumes, 2.6 million periodicals and

1.75 million other serial titles (National Center for Educational Statistics, 1971, p. 3).

As we have indicated earlier, the continuation of miniaturization with videocassettes, cable television, and computer index and retrieval systems may ultimately make it possible for persons to summon printed information on virtually any desired subject to television sets in their own livingrooms.

THE LIBRARY AND THE COMPUTER Levien's study identifies four applications of the computer to library operations: clerical applications, circulation automation, cataloging, and indexing and retrieval.

Clerical applications of the computer have been made in acquisitions and serials control. Although a 1966 survey indicated that less than 200 institutions were thus using the computer for this service (Levien, 1972, in press), Wilcox found that librarians reached by his survey on technology expected library purchasing and circulation management to be substantially automated by 1979 (1972, p. 37).

In the same 1966 survey reported by Levien, it was found that 165 libraries utilized computers in some aspects of circulation automation. Where it is used, it can, among other things, enable a student to use a simple keyboard to enter a book's call number and learn within seconds if it is available or checked out and when it might be back in circulation. At Ohio State University's library of 1 million titles (2.5 million volumes), users may quickly determine through such a system if a book is available and can check it out either in person or by telephone with delivery by campus mail. Starting in September 1972 users of Ohio State's new health center library may ask for a book by a number which an attendant enters on a computer program; the book is removed from a shelf and transported to the desk by an automated system—all within 39 seconds. Michigan State University has implemented a highly automated system with cards for books and for users that can be read by computer data entry devices. The information thus gathered can be used for circulation control (Levien, 1972, in press).

Cataloging is also subject to computerization, although many large and long-established libraries find it expensive because of the costs of converting large existing card holdings to computer-usable forms. New libraries, starting from scratch in their cataloging, can utilize computer capabilities in this process with comparative ease.

The Library of Congress has been providing centralized catalog card preparation services for many years. It now furnishes the service for at least part of its collection through its MARC (MAchine Readable Catalog) computer program in which digitally coded catalog records on magnetic tape are made available to other libraries. Some smaller regional systems are now developing centralized catalog services. Such a service is an essential component of the Ohio College Library Center, which maintains an on-line union list of holdings of libraries throughout the region so that users have access to the combined library resources of the system. The Ohio College Library Center provides catalog cards to over 49 member libraries for a cost of about 3 cents a card.

Indexing and retrieval programs using the computer involve the development of catalog-like information in computer-usable form. At the University of Georgia, bibliographic data stored on magnetic tape by many commercial and governmental agencies is being collected and organized in an experiment to determine the extent to which such data bases can be used by institutions of higher education. At Massachusetts Institute of Technology, a substantial index of literature on structural materials has been compiled for computer storage. The user of the system not only can retrieve bibliographies by subject, author, and title, but also, on command, can have microfiche copies of desired printed pages reproduced on a visual display unit within seconds after their identification.

One interesting feature of the MIT project is its ability to monitor the way in which users take advantage of the program. On the basis of the information provided, it may be possible in the future to reduce the number of key words and phrases that must be programmed to make the system effective.

For MEDLARS, a system created by the National Library of Medicine, indexes of virtually every relevant book, journal, article, and report in bioscience, health, and medicine are prepared for use with a computer. From this data, catalogs of new titles are published monthly and specialized bibliographies are produced on request (Levien, 1972, in press). Personnel at many medical centers throughout the country now have remote access to some of the MEDLARS data through MEDLINE, which connects them to the data base through telephone line hookups.

Librarians responding to the Wilcox survey (1972, p. 37) reported, on the average, that they anticipated "Library users [will] routinely request computerized retrieval of library materials relevant to a particular topic, author, or title" by 1989. They expect that "Library users will be able to 'browse' through most library materials from a remote location with the aid of a computer and visual display terminal" by 2005 (ibid.).

LIBRARIES AS LEARNING CENTERS

Efforts to free libraries from the restraints of a totally print-oriented mission have been underway for many years. The advent of electronic media and new interest in instructional technology have reinforced this interest. One of the main reasons for changes in attitudes on this subject on the nation's campuses has been a realization that the resources of campus libraries (now frequently called *information centers* or *learning-resource centers*) have been inadequately utilized in the instructional efforts of colleges and universities. A manifestation of the new attitude is the physical location of the library at the core of the main instructional facility on several new, small campuses.

A longstanding objection of tradition-bound librarians to the new roles for information centers was breached in 1969 when a joint Committee of the American Association of School Librarians and the Depargment of Audio Visual Instruction of the National Education Association (now the Association for Educational Communications and Technology) issued a report strongly recommending unification of print and nonprint media in "media centers." As one writer said of the report, ". . . the *Standards* recommends a unified media program in which a single institution within the school provides all necessary materials for learning; and quantitatively it prescribes ways for achieving this objective. The words 'library,' 'librarian,' 'audiovisual center' and 'audiovisual specialist' are entirely supplanted by terms such as 'media center' and 'media specialist.' The media center will house *all* learning materials and accompanying services, putting audiovisual and printed resources under an allegedly more favorable single administrative organization and providing easier access for individual or group study" (Burns, 1971, p. 54). The report has been acclaimed widely, but it also has detractors, who are mainly concerned about whether a librarian or audiovisual specialist should be in charge, or whether such an organization should be universally prescribed for all institutions.

Despite such disputes, the Carnegie Commission believes that the library, by whatever name, should occupy a central role in the instructional resources of educational institutions. Its personnel should be available not only for guidance to materials held in the collections of the campus, but also should, when qualified by subject-matter expertise, be utilized as instructors. We also believe that nonprint information, illustrations, and instructional software components should be maintained as part of a unified informational-instructional resource that is cataloged and stored in ways that facilitate convenient retrieval as needed by students and faculty members. Obviously, libraries that assume these additional functions will also face additional costs. Some of these new costs may be offset by consolidating in the library budget those funds that are spent by an institution on existing isolated and independent units which store and distribute learning materials and equipment. Other costs may be incurred, however, as the demand for monprint materials and new services increases, and these costs must be met with new funds.

The question of "who's in charge" of such a facility should be decided by individual institutions.

NETWORKS FOR COMMUNICATIONS AND INFORMATION
Existing libraries and information centers have played a vital role in the formal and informal education of the American people. Until recently, our pattern of independent library establishment serving neighborhoods, communities, schools, colleges, and special interests of various kinds has appeared adequate to the nation's needs, but now the situation has changed. The information revolution has completely overwhelmed some of the smaller and medium-sized library establishments and they have abandoned all hopes of keeping up with it. Moreover, the new technologies for communication and information storage and retrieval involve heavy expenses that many individual libraries cannot afford.

There is also growing concern among librarians for other weaknesses of the nation's library system, including the fact that there is no comprehensive inventory of the nation's information resources (with the result that existing information centers are underutilized). There is also concern for inequities in the delivery of information services (Becker, 1971, p. 14).

In several locations across the country, public and college libraries are forming regional library networks in response to such problems. In higher education, the Ohio College Library Center and the New England Library Network are significant examples. Preliminary plans and proposals for such networks have been made in other parts of the country. To the degree that these networks become effective, they make the information resources of large libraries available to small colleges with limited budgets. They also give colleges and universities a stronger, united voice in claims for rights of access to communications media controlled by government, and more financial capability to adopt advanced information and communications technologies.

As long as the organizational framework of such networks provides those individual institutions with superior collections with adequate compensation for the use of their holdings (possibly by users' fees), we believe that information and communications networks are a logical answer to many of the problems now facing college and university libraries. Moreover, we regard such networks to be, potentially, the hubs of instructional networks in higher education that should soon be organized on a regional level.

5. The Penetration of the New Technology

No one seems to know how extensively the various media for instruction are actually used by institutions of higher education. In 1963, and again in 1967, James W. Brown and James W. Thornton, Jr., of San Jose State College, compiled descriptions of new uses of media in colleges and universities. In the latter compilation, they collected data from 681 of the 1,400 colleges and universities they contacted. Since their original sample represented about half of the colleges and universities in the country, it might be reasonable to assume that between 1,000 and 1,500 colleges and universities were engaged in new media activities of some kind at the time of their survey. Conceivably, an unknown number of other institutions were engaged in media usage, but not in any remarkably "new" way.

Brown and Thornton report a variety of media uses, ranging from limited applications of a single medium to complex combinations of several media and highly sophisticated programs using the computer and television. But, on the whole, it is obvious that the use of informational technology in American higher education is still a largely ad hoc enterprise, advancing unsystematically in response to the enthusiasms and achievements of certain devoted practitioners and the occasional emergence of promising new devices.

Estimates of the date of "maturation" of instructional technology by experts who have been watching for some time have been indefinite. For one thing, it is difficult to define what "maturity" might be.

In January 1972, Jarrod W. Wilcox of the Alfred P. Sloan School of Management at the Massachusetts Institute of Technology made a preliminary report on a study that, among other things, sought to estimate the dates of developments in underlying basic technologies for instruction. Nine technologies were defined as follows:

Routine audiovisual techniques   The classroom use of films, taped lectures shown on closed-circuit television or in listening laboratories, etc.

Programmed instruction   The student uses a text or simple supplementary device which employs step-by-step feedback reinforcement techniques to progress through sequentially ordered, structured material. Examples are programmed texts and self-study language audiotapes.

Routine computer-assisted instruction   The computer is used in the instructional process for either computerized programmed instruction or for drill and practice exercises.

Computer simulation   The computer is used in exercises involving student investigation of the properties of a "pseudo-reality" generated by a model of the phenomenon under study.

Advanced computer-assisted instruction   The computer is used in a flexible, individualized way to support student exploration of a well-defined body of knowledge; this may include Socratic dialogue, tutorial exercises, and the ability to answer at least some unforeseen student questions.

Computer-managed instruction   Measures of the student's performance are monitored and analyzed by the computer; based on this the computer provides aid or direction to the student or teacher as to the most suitable packet of instructional material, such as film, programmed instruction, or live teacher, to be used next.

Remote classroom broadcasting and response   The use of remote television broadcasting from a central location to dispersed classrooms, with at least audio-live response or questions from the students.

Student-initiated access to audiovisual recordings   The use of audiovisual recordings in a technological environment sufficiently inexpensive and easy to use to allow individual student-initiated access to recorded lectures or demonstration material.

Computer-aided course design   The use of computers to record and analyze student responses to instructional packets in computer-assisted and computer-managed instruction in order to provide information for the design of improvements in the instructional material.

Some version of every one of the above basic technologies is already in use in at least one college or university in the country.

In the MIT study, 90 technologists who had participated in various national conferences on educational technology and 152 faculty members representing a broad national cross section of views chose dates by which the nine basic technologies would be in "routine use." The results are summarized in Table 1.

Although the faculty members predicted that six of the nine technologies will be widely available in their fields by 1980, they expected only two of them—routine audiovisual technology and

TABLE 1   *Faculty mean predictions of availability and routine undergraduate and graduate use, and technologists' mean predictions of routine use of nine basic technologies*

	Faculty predictions of availability	*Technologists' predictions of routine use*	*Faculty predictions of routine use for undergraduates*	*Faculty predictions of routine use for graduates*
Routine audiovisual technology	1972	1974	1975	1989
Programmed instruction	1975	1976	1982	2010
Routine computer-assisted instruction	1977	1979	1982	1992
Computer simulation	1979	1979	1983	1985
Advanced computer-assisted instruction	1984	1989	1992	1996
Computer-managed instruction	1986	1983	1995	2005
Remote classroom feedback	1974	1979	1984	1996
Student-initiated access to audiovisual	1975	1979	1979	1986
Computer-aided course design	1983	1983	1992	2003

SOURCE: Wilcox, 1972.

student-initiated access to audiovisual materials — to be in routine use in their own fields at their own institutions by that time. They do not expect advanced computer-assisted instruction, computer-managed instruction, or computer-aided course design to be routinely used in their own fields at their own institutions until at least 1992. Technologists predicted that six of the nine technologies would be in routine use before 1980 and that all of them would be in routine use by 1990.

The faculty expected only two technologies — computer simulation and student-initiated access to audiovisual materials — to be used routinely in graduate instruction before 1990. In several subjects, graduate students are already making sophisticated use of the computer in their instruction — particularly in simulating factors of processes they may be studying. They also are already entrusted with considerably more independence in their learning than are undergraduates. But they are not deeply engaged in the tutorial use of computers Wilcox measured. The close relationship that is considered traditional between the graduate student and his faculty-mentor is not conducive to the use of technology, and incentives to introduce technology to cope with mass instruction do not readily apply in the graduate division. Finally, if concern for instructional objectives dominates technological developments for the next few decades, those developments may not have immediate relevance for graduate study where the objectives are student selected and highly individualized. There is nothing inherent in the new technologies, however, that rules out application to instruction at the graduate level.

On the basis of his general findings, Wilcox concludes that "only those technologies well within the current state of the art are foreseen by faculty as destined for adoption within the next 15 years" (1972, pp. 28–29). He did find, however, that the faculties of larger institutions (over 10,000 students) expect adoption of instructional technology sooner than those at smaller institutions. Despite this latter finding, our impression from site visits and a review of the literature is that the new technologies are now in use at small as well as large colleges. Indeed, but not entirely surprisingly, some of the institutions that have most thoroughly integrated technology into their educational programs are relatively small.

In several studies, there are indications of the degree to which technology will be utilized in different disciplines. For closed-circuit television, we have the 1967 findings (summarized in Table

2) of the Department of Audiovisual Instruction of the National Education Association. There we find usage indicated by 19 academic and 2 professional subject fields. Most frequent use was in education and speech and drama, followed by the life sciences and English. General findings were that the most frequent usages of closed-circuit television were for student self-observation via tapes (202 schools) and observation of others (186 schools) (Depart-

TABLE 2
Use of closed circuit television in higher education by subject area

	Number of institutions reporting use		
	Lower division	*Upper division*	*Graduate*
Subject area			
Agriculture	9	2	2
Business administration	36	23	7
Economics	28	8	1
Education	73	129	78
Engineering	33	32	18
English	71	36	5
Fine arts	63	41	13
Foreign language	34	17	5
History	43	20	2
Humanities	47	22	9
Health/physical education	62	32	5
Life sciences	83	36	14
Mathematics	44	14	7
Military training	11	12	3
Political science	29	16	4
Physical science	71	30	7
Social science	95	49	24
Speech and drama	123	96	28
Technical and vocational	38	20	11
Professional			
Dental			47
Law		1	6
Medical			63
Nursing	1	1	58
Theology			14

SOURCE: Department of Audiovisual Instruction, National Education Association, *A Survey of Institutional Closed Circuit Television,* 1967, pp. 34–35.

ment of Audiovisual Instruction, 1967, p. 38). For computer-assisted instruction, we have more recent results of a survey of California institutions reported by Comstock (1972, in press). Not surprisingly, it was found that engineering accounted for the greatest use of the computer in routine instruction, with computer science, and business and commerce following. Together, engineering, computer science, and business and commerce account for 84 percent of undergraduate students and 73 percent of undergraduate expenditures in instruction using the computers; 52 percent of graduates and 54 percent of graduate expenditures; and 81 percent of all students and 67 percent of all expenditures (Table 3). Appreciable activity was also found in mathematics, physical sciences, social sciences, psychology, education, and agriculture and forestry.

TABLE 3 *Distribution of students and expenditures for instructional computer use, by academic field, 1966–67 (percent of total students and expenditures in each field)**

| | Level of instruction | | | | | |
| | Undergraduates | | Graduates | | Total | |
Field	Students	Expenditures	Students	Expenditures	Students	Expenditures
Engineering	35.2	23.9	33.0	25.7	34.9	24.5
Computer science	23.2	28.5	16.3	14.6	22.2	24.0
Business/commerce	26.0	20.3	2.6	13.2	22.6	18.0
Mathematical subjects	2.2	15.3	12.8	7.0	3.7	12.6
Physical sciences	4.8	3.7	8.2	16.3	5.3	7.8
Social sciences	2.6	2.2	7.4	4.8	3.3	3.0
Psychology	1.2	1.8	3.2	4.2	1.5	2.6
Education	0.9	1.3	6.8	3.9	1.8	2.2
Agriculture/forestry	1.3	0.9	3.6	3.8	1.7	1.8
Biological sciences	0.8	0.7	1.3	2.8	0.9	1.4
Health professions	0.1	0.2	3.1	2.4	0.6	1.0
Humanities/folklore	0.4	0.5	0.5	0.5	0.4	0.5
Military science	0.1	0.3			0.1	0.2
Architecture/city planning	0.3	0.1	0.6	0.3	0.4	0.2
English/journalism	0.1	0.1	0.4	0.1	0.1	0.1
Law	0	0	0.01	0.2	0	0.1
Home economics	0.6	0	0.03	0.1	0.5	0.05
TOTALS	100.0	100.0	100.0	100.0	100.0	100.0

* Summed figures may not equal 100.0 because of rounding.

SOURCE: Levien, 1972, at press.

In an examination of plans for instructional use, Comstock found that in all but two areas, the humanities–liberal arts and teacher preparation, a majority of nonusers have taken definite steps toward computer use. Even in these two areas, more than 40 percent of the nonusers have, at the minimum, begun discussion of the problem (ibid.).

In the Wilcox study, disciplines were grouped under three headings: Liberal and Fine Arts, Business and Education, and Engineering and Science. Faculty in business and education were the most optimistic about future use of technology in their fields, but were seldom more than two or three years ahead of faculty in engineering and science on two degrees of impact—availability of technologies in their field generally and routine use of technologies for undergraduate instruction. There were wider gaps between these two groups of disciplines on the impact levels of graduate instruction and on the possibility that technology would supplant the teacher in some courses. The greatest pessimism at all degrees of impact was expressed by teachers in the liberal and fine arts.

6. Directions for New Effort

In this report, the Carnegie Commission on Higher Education is urging that colleges and universities, industry, governments, and foundations concerned with educational endeavors make an effort to advance the time when currently available technologies will be fully utilized for the instruction of our youth and the continuing education of our citizens. Among the reasons we consider such an effort both desirable and urgent are the following:

1 Expanding technology can enrich the content of students' learning experiences, provide greater flexibility and variety in the organization of instruction, and give students a more self-reliant role in their own education.

2 An enormous investment has already been made in experimentation and research with instructional technology in the United States. The investment of the national government alone in such endeavors was more than $2.5 billion between 1966 and 1969 (Molnar, 1969). The technology and know-how that have emerged from these efforts are, to a considerable extent, available for application, but defects in communicating results of experiments to institutions, and inadequate incentives and procedures for effective development, distribution, and utilization of new instructional programs, keep them from general use. Prudence dictates making an early effort to begin to capitalize on the investments we have already made.

3 Although short-run costs for the development and introduction of new instructional technology are expected to be very great, they will ultimately yield dividends. Much of the expanding technology has the potential economic effect of spreading the benefit of investment in a single unit of instruction among very large numbers of

students. It therefore has an ability to increase the productivity of higher education. The earlier efforts are made to develop the expanding instructional technology fully, the earlier this increased productivity will be realized.

4 College enrollments are now declining and will stabilize in the 1980s, but they will begin to rise again in the 1990s. By investing faculty resources now—when they are in relative abundance—in the development and introduction of instructional programs using expanded technologies, we can reduce to some extent the need in years to come to expand physical facilities and faculties to accommodate rising enrollments in the 1990s.

5 Several distinct but possibly converging trends in the development and organization of new technologies for use in higher education are discernable. Among them are efforts to reduce the costs of using the most expensive technologies by arranging for interinstitutional cooperation, the development of joint or regional library networks, and the utilization of computing for a variety of tasks that cut across instructional, administrative, and research functions. At the same time that these trends are emerging, the new technology is being utilized by individual institutions on a somewhat haphazard or uneven basis. There is a much better chance that the benefits of instructional technology will be effectively and fully utilized if its introduction and development are coordinated and planned than if it is allowed to follow its present, largely uncontrolled course. Coordination and planning will be easier now, when considerable flexibility still exists, than it will be later when current divergent directions of development become rigidly fixed.

Recommendation 1: Because expanding technology will extend higher learning to large numbers of people who have been unable to take advantage of it in the past, because it will provide instruction in forms that will be more effective than conventional instruction for some learners in some subjects, because it will be more effective for all learners and many teachers under many circumstances, and because it will significantly reduce costs of higher education in the long run, its early advancement should be encouraged by the adequate commitment of colleges and universities to its utilization and development and by adequate support from governmental and other agencies concerned with the advancement of higher learning.

PRODUCING MORE LEARNING MATERIALS One of the great disappointments of the national effort to date is that for all the funds and effort thus far expended for the advancement of instructional technology, penetration of new learning materials and media into higher education has thus far been shallow. Even relatively commonplace technologies are not in evidence on many campuses. Equipment that has been installed at some institutions has fallen into disuse or is utilized to only a fraction of its capacity.

We cannot argue that the existing technology is perfect. The list of desirable improvements is long, including more compatible systems and components produced by manufacturers; "bug-free" terminals and learning stations that are used for access to computer service or audiovisual communication; faster techniques for student communication with computers; more extensive two-way communications capacities in instructional systems using electronic media; and effective character reading equipment to assist in indexing and cataloging information. There is admittedly much development work to be done. But there is also a remarkable amount of operational technology available for use.

What seems to be needed now is somewhat less financial support for invention of equipment and more financial support for the development and utilization of what we already have. If our aim is to have technology follow instructional needs, high priority must be placed, during the next two decades, upon the design and utilization of effective instructional programs suitable for use or adaptation by more than one institution. We have been told by one informed observer of computer development that out of the hundreds of instructional programs for computer use that have been so far designed, only about half a dozen are regarded as suitable for transport beyond the institution where they were developed. A similar plight characterizes instructional materials designed for other media.

We would urge, in this regard, that at the same time institutions encourage their faculties to engage in efforts to create and improve instructional materials, they also encourage their faculty members to introduce, as it may be appropriate, available instructional units devised by others. In itself, reliance on instruction of one's own design is not a pure virtue. To utilize poorly designed materials when better ones are available is shortsighted. It deprives students of exposure to instructional components that may be of superior quality; it deprives professors themselves of opportunities to enrich instruction or to extend the time they can place at their institution's disposal; and, in the long view, it restrains development of market forces that need to exist if the benefits of a mature instructional technology are to be realized.

The introduction of technology into education should be accompanied by a deliberate effort of all concerned to set and maintain high standards of quality for the materials used. Institutions of higher education themselves should be particularly interested and involved in such an effort. We have also been impressed by activities of certain academic disciplines—notably physics and mathematics—in the improvement of instruction and learning materials.

Recommendation 2: <u>Since a grossly inadequate supply of good quality instructional materials now exists, a major thrust of financial support and effort on behalf of instructional technology for the next decade should be toward the development and utilization of outstanding instructional programs and materials. The academic disciplines should follow the examples of physics and mathematics in playing a significant role in such efforts.</u>

THE NEED FOR HIGHER EDUCATION'S LEADERSHIP The impetus for the early development of instructional technology that was strong in the late 1950s and 1960s has subsided in recent years. One of the problems seems to be that leadership and focus for the effort have been lacking. And the reasons are fairly clear:

1 Industry, which generated much of the current instructional technology as a spin-off from developments originally intended for use by business, scientific research, and communications industries, is unable to devote large-scale efforts to advance educational technology. The director of Educational Products Information Exchange Institute in New York estimates that in all of education in the United States only $2 or $3 billion a year (higher education's share would be about $500 million) are available after salaries and maintenance expenditures for instructional materials (Komoski, 1970, 1, p. 907). He expressed doubt that such a small market would support full-throttle competition of very many companies for the development of technologies specifically designed for educational use. As a result, industry is concentrating on the production and sales of such instructional technologies as have already proved their sales potential in the market place.

2 As we shall indicate more fully later in this section, the federal government has been a promising source of initiative for at least

two decades and has made very generous financial contributions for the support of research, development, and applications of instructional media and learning systems. But the federal government has been in many respects too remote from individual institutions of higher education and has had no means of securing their general participation in the needed effort.

3 Colleges and universities have been unable to take the initiative because they have been operating for several years with severely constricted budgets. New institutions may be able to incorporate new technologies into their instructional programs on both economical and instructional grounds. But many existing institutions are able to invest in the new technologies only if they promise immediate cost-savings. Moreover, the apathy and, in many instances, the resistance faculty members feel toward the adoption of new instructional technologies have deterred colleges and universities from moving confidently into a leadership role.

No one segment of our society—industry, government, or higher education—will be able to bring about the full and effective use of instructional technology alone. They each have an important role to play. But higher education clearly has a great stake in the outcome of the effort and should endeavor to protect it by exercising whatever influence it possibly can. Because the admittedly large costs that initially will be incurred for such activity will ultimately be offset by greater productivity, we feel that the greatest obstacle to higher educations's accepting a leadership role is the lack of institutional commitment.

THE COMMITMENT NEEDED BY INSTITUTIONS On too many campuses in the United States a handful of instructors, and occasionally an isolated department, develop enthusiasms for specific media or devices. Their successes are inadequately communicated to the rest of the campuses; their failures are ignored. On some campuses, officials who are responsible for maintaining instructional equipment are regarded as gadget fans, and the procedures for the use of instructional equipment have become so bureaucratic that they discourage utilization.

On at least one campus where instructional technology has been effectively (and economically) introduced with due consideration for its impacts on the total academic enterprise, the responsibility resides in the college's top academic officer. Such officers should be able to call upon the expertise of instructional departments, librarians, technologists, and others on the campus who are able to contribute advice and skills to the improvement of the instructional process. We therefore believe that the authority for developing instructional technology in its broadest form should be placed high in the academic organization of the institutions, should be exercised as a part of responsibilities for instructional quality generally, and should not be so isolated from the main tent of instructional policy making and practice that it is an education sideshow.

To create a proper environment for utilization of the new technology, therefore, the following steps are necessary:

1 An institution should demonstrate its commitment to effective instruction. In a forthcoming report on new academic developments in higher education, we will discuss the roles of deans of undergraduate instruction in setting the standards and spreading the gospel of quality instruction. Where such officers do not now exist, perhaps they should be appointed, and among their responsibilities for mobilizing their institutions' total instructional resources should be concern for the effective utilization of technology. Under their auspices, information about instructional technology should be maintained and made available to faculty members. They should arrange training sessions for faculty members interested in developing learning materials that utilize advanced media and procedures. They should serve as campus liaison with governments, foundations, and other sources of financial support for introducing promising innovations in the utilization of new media and techniques. They should assume responsibility for identifying effective uses of technology on campus and, when appropriate, for calling it to the attention of the total faculty and of regional, national, or professional organizations engaged in the development and distribution of educational materials.

2 Institutions should, to whatever degree their resources permit, make the new technologies available for use on the campus. In some instances, they may not be able to provide expensive facilities themselves, but can arrange for sharing them through participation in consortia or other cooperative programs. Institutions should make every effort to plan new buildings so that they will be fully adaptive to the use of new technologies. Adequate wiring and provision for potential 24-hour use of facilities are minimal parts of that capability.

3 Finally, institutions should provide adequate professional assistance to faculty members engaged in the development of instruction utilizing advanced media.

Recommendation 3: Institutions of higher education should contribute to the advancement of instructional technology not only by giving favorable consideration to expanding its use, whenever such use is appropriate, but also by placing responsibility for its introduction and utilization at the highest possible level of academic administration.

THE ROLE OF LIBRARIES

In Section 4, we stated our belief that the library should occupy a central role in the instructional resources of educational institutions. We also noted there that considerable progress has been made by libraries in introducing automation into their operations; in developing networks for the sharing of catalogs and collections by many institutions; and in accommodating films, recordings, tapes, and other nonprint materials in systematically organized storage and retrieval systems. Although, as is the case with most of the new technology, the advancement of information science by using new media and equipment is young and uneven, it has produced impressive results in several significant instances. We therefore regard libraries as promising catalysts of continuing innovation and development in the use of technology by colleges and universities.

Beyond that conclusion, we consider knowledge itself to be the essence of any learning experience, and we regard the libraries and information centers charged with preserving knowledge in the increasingly variable forms in which it can be recorded as indispensable components of any effort to fully utilize instructional technology.

Recommendation 4: The introduction of new technologies to help libraries continue to improve their services to increasing numbers of users should be given first priority in the efforts of colleges and universities, government agencies, and other agencies seeking to achieve more rapid progress in the development of instructional technology.

THE ROLE OF EXTRAMURAL EDUCATION

We hope that in coming decades interest and effort in the use and development of instructional technology will be demonstrated generally by all types of institutions of higher learning, including community colleges, liberal arts colleges, comprehensive colleges, and universities; they cannot remain unaffected by instructional technology forever. But a realistic appraisal of current progress suggests that the most significant advances, in the coming decade, at least, will be generated by emerging institutions and extramural educational systems that are being created alongside traditional ones. They are primarily designed to provide education for working adults or young students for whom attendance in regular college or university classrooms is neither feasible nor desirable. Some of these systems will rely heavily upon the model provided by the Open University in Great Britain. Although traditional institutions may employ the new technologies for 10 to 20 percent of their instruction by the year 2000, extramural education may use them for up to 80 percent of their instruction.

The characteristics of such alternative systems that make them especially well-suited for a role in the development of instructional technology are the following:

- They are new, and not tradition-bound.

- They must, by their very nature, develop learning materials that are largely self-instructing.

- They are, to a considerable extent, mass-oriented, drawing their students from an extremely wide spectrum within American society and, potentially, in very great numbers. This characteristic will enable them to utilize services of individual faculty members in an extremely efficient way.

- They are physically without boundaries. Their students may be located at considerable distance from the base of operations and from each other.

- They are not subject to the time restraints imposed by traditional college calendars.

These characteristics imply a considerable tolerance for innovation, the need for instructional materials of some variety, and uses of communications that have the felicitous quality of becoming less expensive as student bodies increase. For that reason, extramural education systems are likely to provide a relatively early market for instructional materials that utilize two-way cable television capacities, videocassettes, time-sharing computer facilities, remote-control access to audiovisual presentations, and centralized information storage centers.

With the experience of the Open University of Great Britain as an example, extramural education systems will be well-served by making a commitment to give careful attention to the development of learning materials. The minimum of six-months to one-year planning time utilized for each course in the Open University has proved well spent. The involvement of carefully balanced planning teams in the design of instructional units has been of great value.

Quality of instruction in the extramural education programs is vital to the advance of successful uses of educational technology because these systems offer a natural bridge between research and development and practical application. If they are successful in their innovations and in their utilization of the new technologies, these systems are likely to challenge traditional institutions to attempt more innovation. We therefore believe that extramural education systems should recieve particular (though not exclusive) consideration for financial support for their efforts to advance instructional technology.

Recommendation 5: We recommend that major funding sources, including states, the federal government, and foundations, recognize not only the potential of new and developing extramural education systems for expanding learning opportunities, but also the crucial role such systems should play in the ultimate development of instructional technologies. Requests of these systems for funds with which to introduce and use new instructional programs, materials, and media should be given favorable consideration.

COOPERATIVE
LEARNING-
TECHNOLOGY
CENTERS

Although we believe that federal resources must be available for the encouragement of development in instructional technology, we do not consider it desirable or wise for the federal government to dominate such endeavors. Caution in the centralization of effort becomes especially prudent as the direction of activity shifts to embrace the content of instructional programs and the quality of instructional delivery programs. At the other extreme, we do not feel that the nation has yet realized satisfactory results from the widely diffused efforts of individual institutions and agencies. Diversified and scattered individual projects must, in some way, be focused for effective impact.

A reasonable alternative to these extremes is a system of cooperative learning-technology centers that are regionally organized and, ideally, interstate in dimension. Thus constituted, these centers would have reasonably large service areas affording to participating institutions the benefits of spreading costs of constructing and acquiring expensive mediaware and facilities among many users. Operating expenses per capita for the centers should decrease as the number of users increase.

Recommendation 6: By 1992, at least seven cooperative learning-technology centers, voluntarily organized on a regional basis by participating higher educational institutions and systems should be established for the purpose of sharing costs and facilities for the accelerated development and utilization of instructional technology in higher education.

We suggest that formation of such centers take place with the following metropolitan areas as focal points:

- Atlanta
- Boston
- Chicago
- Denver
- Houston
- Philadelphia
- San Francisco

One possible configuration of such regional districts is suggested on Map 1.

By suggesting these focal points, we do not mean to imply that all of the facilities of the cooperative learning-technology centers should be physically located in any one city. In fact, we believe that in any of the proposed learning-technology centers services can, and perhaps should, be rendered from more than one location. It would seem particularly wise to include as part of the center's total system the most fully developed library, computing, communications, and extramural instruction networks that already exist in the district. As long as the basic integrity of the learning-technology center is respected by having all four of these fundamental facilities as a part of its endeavors, the physical location of the various components can be dispersed.

Initiative for the formation of cooperative learning-technology centers might be taken by individual institutions; by existing computer, communications, or library networks; or by regional education associations. Individual states in which most of a learning-technology center's essential facilities are in a state of advanced

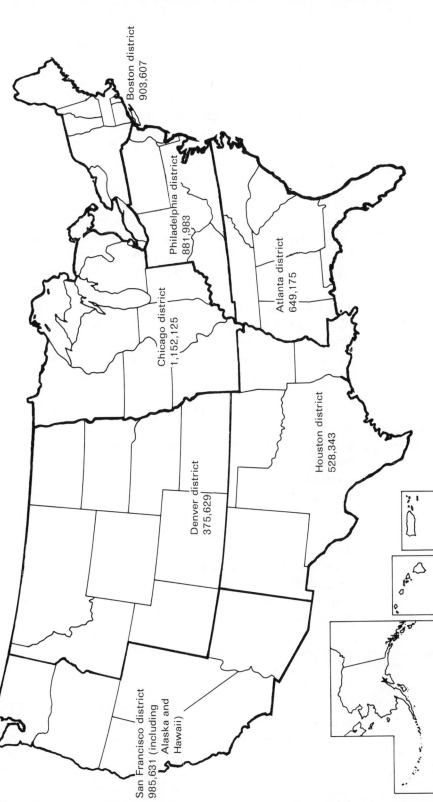

MAP 1 Suggested configuration of districts that might be served by cooperative learning-technology centers, with indication of numbers of under-graduate students (1968) in each

Boston district
903,607

Philadelphia district
881,983

Atlanta district
649,175

Chicago district
1,152,125

Houston district
528,343

Denver district
375,629

San Francisco district
985,631 (including
Alaska and
Hawaii)

NOTE: Enrollment data from Carnegie Commission on Higher Education, 1971, pp. 134–135.

development might well take initiative in the formation of such centers. The states of New York, Illinois, and California are among those that could consider generating such a movement. Organizations such as the Western Interstate Commission for Higher Education (WICHE) and the Southern Regional Educational Board (SREB), which are already organized on a multi-institutional, multistate basis might also sponsor development of learning-technology centers.

Functions of Cooperative Learning-Technology Centers

Unlike the regional laboratories and the research and development centers created by the federal government to work independently in the discovery and testing of new types of instruction based on an expanding technology, the proposed cooperative learning-technology centers would be service units for participating institutions. They could engage in research and development activity, but would be required to devote most of their efforts to the identification, production, and distribution of already developed teaching and learning materials that are appropriate for college instruction. They would also make available to their members centralized computing, information, and large-scale production facilities that would be too expensive for individual institutions to provide for themselves. They should be regional clearinghouses for information about the availability and use of new instructional materials. They should be able to provide professional expertise for the development of new instructional materials utilizing all the available media—and most particularly computers, television, film, and audio- and videocassettes. They might also serve as another link between faculty members who have developed promising instructional materials and government, foundations, and industry. Cooperative learning-technology centers should affiliate with one or more extramural educational systems within their service areas so that they may actively engage in instructional as well as developmental and service activities.

Components of Cooperative Learning-Technology Centers

Each cooperative learning-technology center should have four components:

Production unit This unit would be responsible for the design, planning, and production of instructional units for use by participating institutions and extramural education systems within the jurisdiction of the center. It would also develop and control centralized facilities for its activities. It may also subcontract some of its work to private industry or individual institutions.

Resource unit This unit would be a library and information system organized for regional service. It would organize and administer interlibrary loan services and would catalog both print and nonprint materials available at institutions within the center's jurisdiction. It would also catalog and store print and nonprint materials prepared under the sponsorship of the center itself. It would utilize the most fully automated systems feasible for cataloging, indexing, and information retrieval and provide regional leadership in the development of modern interlibrary communications and information services adaptable to the needs of institutional libraries and informational subsystems.

Distribution unit This unit should be actively engaged in instructional activity through one or more extramural educational systems directly, and indirectly, as needed, by other member institutions. It should have faculties and staff members responsible for the design, conduct, and evaluation of teaching and learning segments in a substantial number of course offerings.

Computing unit This unit would provide the core storage for computer programs used by the region, and offer on-line computing services for instructional management, administration, and instructional computer use for the cooperative learning-technology center and its participants.

Funding Cooperative Learning-Technology Centers The funding for cooperative learning-technology centers should be provided from three sources:

1 Because they will require certain facilities that they cannot provide entirely by themselves, they will need support from the federal government. Federal incentives for the organization of cooperative learning-technology centers could include grants for construction; loans for teaching, learning, and communications equipment that can be amortized through user charges; and grants for the development of instructional materials. We believe that the federal government should provide all the initial capital expenses.

It should also provide at least one-third of the operating expenditures for each cooperative learning-technology center during its first decade of operations.

Recommendation 7: The federal government should assume full financial responsibility for the capital expenditures required initially to establish one cooperative learning-technology center every three years between 1973 and 1992.

Recommendation 8: The federal government should provide at least one-third of the funds required for the operation of cooperative learning-technology centers for the first ten years of their operation.

To qualify for federal assistance, we believe that cooperative learning-technology centers should provide evidence of a plan to serve at least 200,000 students and show efforts to organize one or more regional library systems, one or more operating computer time-sharing programs, and one or more extramural educational systems.

2 Participating institutions should share the cost of the development and operation of cooperative learning-technology center facilities (perhaps initially utilizing the best existing facilities at participating institutions). Student fees could offset some instructional expense and provide reserves for use in acquiring new mediaware, as it improves, for institutional applications. Basic operating expenses of the information unit and computer unit could be shared on a re-charge or some other equitable basis agreed upon by participating members.

3 The centers should also be encouraged to seek short-term special-project support from governments, foundations, and industry. They might also consider charging fees or royalties on the use of instructional materials created by their own staffs or member institutions but adapted for national production and distribution.

Governance of Cooperative Learning-Technology Centers We have stressed the voluntary nature of cooperative learning-technology centers. In so doing, we are fully aware that such organizations are extremely difficult to establish and govern. Participating members will have different sizes, different functions, and different objectives. Some participants will have more resources to invest in the cooperative effort than others will. And there will inevitably be varying expectations—some of which are in conflict. There is an added complication that arises from the fact that an attempt must be made not only to achieve cooperation of institutions, but also to accomplish the convergence of heretofore independent efforts in the advancement of instructional technology by such divergent groups as audiovisual specialists, computer scientists, librarians, radio and television technicians, behavioral scientists, and academics. Assuring that participating institutions and relevant interests are fairly represented in the governance of each center will require at minimum a fundamental commitment on the part of all concerned to the achievement of the benefits that concerted effort can realize.

The precise governing structure of each cooperative learning-technology center should be determined by the members themselves. We would suggest, however, that operating authority should be entrusted to an individual director assisted by a relatively small committee of persons equitably representative not only of the main types of member colleges and universities but also of the four major activity components involved in the center's program.

Wherever possible, existing facilities of participating institutions should be utilized.

Initially, we believe that the services of the centers should be restricted to institutions of higher education. Ultimately, however, appropriate instructional materials developed by the centers could be made available to elementary and secondary schools, public libraries, and other types of institutions in the region.

Estimated Costs of Cooperative Learning-Technology Centers

Because there are so few precedents to follow, and so many variables to consider, it is difficult to estimate costs of cooperative learning-technology centers very firmly. However, by combining cost figures on operations comparable to those of the envisaged components of the proposed center, the following estimates are obtained for one center:

- Initial capital investment: $35 million
- Annual operating expenses: $150 million

Capital investment includes $15 million for converting existing catalog card indexes to computer-usable forms, and $20 million for physical facilities to house center library materials and communications and instructional operations.

Capital expenses will be reduced to the extent that adequate facilities already exist and are available for use by all member institutions in a region.

Operating costs include $100 million for central computer operations, $20 million for television and film materials production, $10 million for course planning and other instructional activities, and $20 million for library and information center activities. The operating cost figures do not include costs of individual computer terminals, which would presumably be provided by participating institutions.

GENERAL
EFFORTS
BY THE
FEDERAL
GOVERNMENT

The federal government has been supporting research, development, and utilization of instructional technology for at least two decades.

To facilitate information exchange in the instructional technology field, the Office of Education sponsors the ERIC Clearinghouse at Stanford, established in 1964, which organizes and disseminates information on instructional films, television, programmed instruction, computer-assisted instruction, and other audiovisual means of teaching. The Office of Education also supports Educational Products Information Exchange (EPIE), created in 1966, which serves as a central agency to "evaluate, codify, and disseminate reliable information about instructional media and instrumentation" (Saettler, 1968, p. 351). We believe that the existence and availability of these information services should be made more widely known to institutions of higher education—where the movement for the advancement of instructional technology suffers most for lack of awareness of current developments.

The Office of Education is also the financial sponsor for Regional Educational Research and Development Centers which were created under Title IV of the Elementary and Secondary Education Act of 1965 and which were charged with responsibilities for research, surveys, and demonstrations in the field of education including, "discovering and testing new educational ideas (including new uses of printed and audiovisual media) and more effective educational practices and putting into use those which show promise of success." Initially, 20 regional laboratories and 8 R&D Centers were created under this and prior legislation. The number of laboratories has been reduced to 11 (Levien, 1972, in press).

In 1968, Congress enacted a series of amendments to the Higher Educational Facilities Act of 1963. Among them was legislation creating "Networks for Knowledge," a plan to encourage colleges and universities to share, through cooperative arrangements, their technical and other educational and administrative facilities and resources. It provided for the granting of funds for projects that included joint uses of classrooms, libraries, laboratories, books, materials, or equipment; access to specialized library collections through interinstitutional catalogs and suitable media for electronic or other rapid transmission facilities; and establishment and joint operation of electronic computer networks and programs. Authorizations of $340,000 for the first year, $4 million for the year ending June 30, 1970, and $15 million for the year ending June 30, 1971, were enacted, but none of these funds were ever appropriated.

We believe that the financial initiative for the development and application of the new technologies remains with the federal government, probably through the year 2000. Of all possible funding agencies, the federal government has the largest fund resources to draw upon. Moreover, the development of instructional technology promises quality and financial benefits to all of education, not just to certain kinds of institutions or only to institutions in certain areas of the country.

The "Educational Technology Act of 1969" (H.R. 8838) would authorize $300 million for the support of educational technology — $200 million in elementary and secondary education and $100 million in higher education (Grayson, 1972, p. 1220). We believe that a federal expenditure at that level is minimal for support of educational technology in higher education and recommend that at least $100 million be provided for the support of well-targeted educational technology utilization in 1973 and that the level of federal expenditure for such purposes should increase to at least 1 percent of the total national expenditures for higher education in the United States ($25 billion in 1970–71) by 1980.

Federal funds should be used, as in the past, to support research and development activity in the general field of instructional technology. However, we believe increasing emphasis should be placed on supporting projects that will result in the actual production and increased utilization of new learning materials and instructional media. Much of this support should go, as it has in the past, to independent associations and institutions and should be awarded on the basis of the merit of project proposals. Some of it will also be needed for the support of the cooperative learning-technology centers recommended in this report.

In supporting both individual projects and projects that fall within the jurisdiction of cooperative learning-technology centers, the federal government should utilize its influence in making grants to encourage the development of teaching and learning materials that can be utilized broadly throughout the country. It should also favor development of materials and processes that are compatible with the broadest possible spectrum of existing models of available media hardware.

Recommendation 9: The federal government should continue to provide a major share of expenditures required for research and development in instructional technology and for introduction of new technologies more extensively into higher education at least until the end of the century. The total level of federal government support for these purposes should be at least $100 million in 1973 and should rise to 1 percent of the total expenditures of the nation on higher education by 1980.

In determining the policies under which federal funds are provided to support the advance of instructional technology, granting agencies should provide particular encouragement for the design and production of materials that can be widely used by institutions throughout the country. Related to that objective is the need for financial encouragement for the development of instructional materials that can be conveniently used with the most widely available or readily adaptable equipment.

Agencies for the Administration of Federal Programs

Two federal agencies that could play important roles in the development of instructional technology in higher education have been proposed.

1 A National Foundation for the Development of Higher Education has been proposed by the Commission to "encourage, advise, review, and provide financial support for institutional programs designed to give new directions in curricula, to strengthen essential areas that have fallen behind or have never been adequately developed because of inadequate funding, and to develop programs for improvement of educational processes and techniques" (Carnegie Commission on Higher Education, 1968, pp. 45–46). A bill

proposing establishment of a National Foundation of Postsecondary Education with functions similar to those outlined in the above proposal is currently pending in Congress. If this agency is established, it would be the most appropriate one for the administration of loans and the provision of capital investment funds and grants for the development and utilization of new instructional materials either by institutions or by cooperative learning-technology centers.

2   The second proposed agency is a National Institute of Education. Its function is to "Conduct and support education R&D, disseminate its findings, train educational R&D personnel, and promote coordination of educational R&D within the Federal Government." If it is established, this agency would be the appropriate one for making grants for research and development (but not implementation) activities in the field of instructional technology in higher education.

Recommendation 10: The proposed National Foundation for Postsecondary Education and the proposed National Institute of Education should be established, and the proposed National Foundation for Postsecondary Education should be assigned responsibility for administering loans and the provision of capital investment funds and grants for the utilization of instructional technology. Grants to support research and development activities in the field of instructional technology for higher education should be made by the proposed National Institute of Education.

In the event neither of these agencies are created, we would propose that the functions in the development of instructional technology we recommend for them could be performed by appropriate agencies of the U.S. Department of Health, Education and Welfare.

THE ROLE OF INDUSTRY   We expect industry to continue to perform its historic role in the advancement of instructional technologies. Its most obvious contributions have been in the production and distribution of both software and mediaware for the new teaching and learning processes. It can also play a role in actively encouraging creative college and university faculty members to develop such materials and can provide some of the rewards to which such persons are entitled in return for their contributions to instructional technology. There is no reason, moreover, why the publishing, entertainment, and communications industries, on their own initiative but with the consultation of educators, cannot also develop instructional materials independently.

In carrying out this role, industry must be aware of a difficult problem that current development and manufacturing practices have posed for educational institutions that attempt to use the new media. The broad generalization that the technology of the fourth revolution already exists is subject to an important caveat—it is available in a variety of forms and styles, many of which are incompatible with one another. One difficulty is that much of the technology has been designed basically for uses in business, industry, or public communications. We believe that greater efforts should be made in the future to develop a technology that meets the special needs of education. Until that happens, however, it is desirable that producers of mediaware make every effort to develop equipment capable of accommodating learning components of considerable variety. The needs for such developments are particularly acute with media that use computer programs, audiotapes, and videocassettes. We hope that the National Bureau of Standards, industrial associations, and other appropriate organizations will fully exercise their influence and enforcement authority to achieve greater compatibility in media that can be used for instruction than is currently prevalent.

LEGAL RESTRAINTS ON DUPLICATION One particularly complicating factor in the development of instructional technology involves copyright protection of printed matter and visual display materials. Here, the best interests of the learner —who needs the widest possible access to materials at a reasonable price—often come into conflict with the best interests of the creative individuals who design the materials and the producers who manufacture them. Equitable resolution of the extremely complex issues involved transcends the subject of this report, but we do believe that when legal restraints upon the duplication of educational materials are thoroughly reviewed by Congress, special attention should be given to the impacts of such restraints on the capabilities and advantages of instruction provided by the new instructional technology.

7. Impacts on Faculty

So much emphasis has been placed upon the importance of technology to the expansion of learning opportunities for students that the impression that teaching-learning media will immediately replace the professor or reduce his importance is widely held.

Such fears are ill-founded. During the 1960s instructional technology was strongly advocated at some institutions as a means of relieving the teaching shortages on campuses threatened by burgeoning enrollments. Pursuant to this rationale, some technology was introduced to colleges and universities during that decade. The objective was not to reduce the size of the faculty, but to make better and fuller use of the capabilities of the short supply of faculty then expected to be available.

That basic objective of better and fuller use of capabilities should prevail today and into the future, and is valid even when faculty supply is abundant. It has obvious applications where the classroom presence of professors is impossible for logistical reasons— for example in extramural degree programs or in remote areas that can be reached conveniently only by books and instruction provided through electronic media. But the function of the new technology should also be to expand the capabilities of instructors. It should relieve them of the need to prepare and personally deliver elementary course segments that change very little from year to year. It should provide them with time-saving ways to drill students in knowledge that must be mastered if the rest of the term's course content is to be fully understood. It should expand the professors' resources for demonstration and illustration. And it should give them more time to prepare their courses, meet with students in small groups, and provide individual counseling. It is impossible to say how much time professors should be able to save using the expanding technology. Some will save none or very little because instructional technology has nothing to offer them. Others can save 50 percent or more of their preparation and classroom time. Zenon Zannetos (1968) at the Sloan School of Management at M.I.T. has devised a computer-instructed segment of a graduate course in accounting that saves a professor about that much time.

But the time-saving features of instructional technology should not be prematurely emphasized. One of the heaviest investments needed immediately in the development of instructional technology is faculty time for development of teaching-learning materials. In their study of efficiency in liberal education, Howard Bowen and Gordon Douglass (1971, p. 27) found that the instructional mode they analyzed that made the most use of technology required some 10 more hours of an instructor's time per week for course preparation than did a conventional instructional mode. A much earlier—1960—study of time spent by faculty members at Miami University in the preparation of television instruction found that faculty members spent from three to six times as much time preparing for an hour of television instruction than they spent preparing for a conventional lecture (Dubin & Hedley, 1969, p. 52). Once instructional materials have been prepared, they must also be periodically revised. And revision of instructional materials for advanced media is much more time-consuming than simply revising a lecture or amending a syllabus. The language of computers is precise and changes in programs to be used with this medium can be slow and tedious. Alterations in films and television tapes may require wholesale duplication in order to avoid reassembling personnel, sets, and equipment used in original versions. Adequate reward systems will be required if faculty members are to be encouraged to engage in such activities.

Recommendation 11: Colleges and universities should provide incentives to faculty members who contribute to the advancement of instructional technology. Released time for the development of instructional materials and promotions and salary improvement for successful achievement in such endeavors should be part of that encouragement.

The need for faculty members to devote time to the design, development, and revision of instructional materials in an extensive way during the coming decade could offset some of the difficulties of a period of declining enrollments in which the number of people prepared for academic careers temporarily exceeds demand. Under these conditions, faculty members may be utilized for the development of new instructional software without adversely affecting the supply of teachers adequately prepared for classroom service. By the end of the 1980s, when the faculty ranks will have stabilized in response to steady or declining student enrollments, we would hope that the availability of instructional materials and expansion of technology use would be such that the rising enrollments of the 1990s could be served without extraordinary faculty increases. During the 1970s and 1980s, however, we do not foresee the development of instructional technology as a major cause of faculty dismissals. It could, in fact, be a factor in reducing the impact of dropping enrollments on faculty employment during that period.

Beginning in the 1980s, however, the effective utilization of instructional technology should have matured to the extent that greater numbers of students can be taught with fewer faculty members than is the case now. At that point the available places for new teachers will become constricted. Professors already employed will either retain their positions or will become absorbed in the emerging instructional professions associated with the development of new teaching and learning materials and procedures.

A NEW ROLE FOR FACULTIES
While we do not believe that the new technology will immediately reduce the number of faculty members we have, it will change their roles significantly. There is no question but that they will and should remain central to the instructional process. Their judgment in selecting teaching and learning materials will have at least the same impact upon the quality of instruction as their selection of textbooks and preparation of recommended reading lists do at the present time. They must continue to be held accountable for the effectiveness of whatever materials are presented in the classroom under their jurisdiction. We believe also that they should be in full command of course preparation and presentation. But we agree with Alvin Eurich (1969, p. 115) that:

The teacher as purveyor of information, as drillmaster, as jack-of-all-trades, is obsolete. His new role, that only technology fully realized can create, will be that of a master of the resources of learning, at last afforded time and opportunity for the cultivation of students as individual human beings with a potential to learn.

In the future, we believe that for at least part of their jobs, professors must become leaders of teams of instructional development personnel. To prepare fully for the new faculty roles, prospective college and university teachers should ideally have training and experience in instructional development and the use of the new technology prior to their first academic appointments. In our report, *Less Time, More Options,* issued in January 1971 (1971*a*), we recommended that the new Doctor of Arts degree offered by some institutions in the United States should be widely accepted as a degree for the "nonresearch teacher." It would require "(*a*) a broader field of basic knowledge than the more specialized Ph.D. degree and (*b*) an opportunity to study and practice pedagogic technique." This recommendation becomes especially urgent if instructional technology is to be fully and wisely utilized. Institutions offering the proposed Doctor of Arts degree or other courses of instruction designed to prepare college and university teachers should provide instruction and experience in course development and the utilization of learning resources and instructional technologies as a part of their curricula.

Institutions training college-level teachers should keep in mind that many of the students they accept in the 1970s will still be in service in the year 2000 when we expect what is now considered new instructional technology will be in general use.

Recommendation 12: Colleges and universities that are responsible for the training of prospective university, college, and high school teachers should begin now to incorporate in their curricula instruction on the development of teaching-learning segments that appropriately utilize the expanding technologies of instruction.

It has been our observation that some of the most impressive progress in instructional technology has been inspired by the initiative of individual faculty members who have grasped the potentials of new techniques and have applied them intelligently to their own teaching. On the other hand, faculty members themselves now rate resistance of faculty as second only to lack of funds as the most severe obstacle to the adoption of the new technologies. In Wilcox's study, "attitudes of the faculty" ranked above "effectiveness of technology," "attitude of students," and "attitude of administrators" as an obstacle (Wilcox, 1972, p. 34). Investigators at the University of Oregon found that faculty members tended to favor instructional television generally (Table 4), but lost their enthusiasm as the possibility that they might themselves become involved in it became more immediate (Table 5) (Dubin & Hedley, 1969, pp. 32, 36).

Much of the resistance of faculty members to the introduction and use of the new technology will be overcome as it becomes more widely available and easier to use. If our suggestions earlier in this report that appropriate use of instructional technology should be introduced into the programs designed to prepare men and women for college-level teaching are adopted, more and more young faculty

TABLE 4
Professors are more favorable than unfavorable toward ETV

QUESTION: What is your feeling about television instruction generally?*

Source-study number	Year of study	Academic institution	N	Favorable	Neutral	Unfavorable
28 (p. 49)	1959	Oregon College of Education	28	75%	11%	14%
		Oregon State University†	171	62	18	20
		University of Oregon	123	58	21	21
		Willamette University	26	42	15	43
29 (p. 32)	1961	University of Minnesota	892	47	42	11
13 (Appendix., Table 3)	1962	University of Houston	117	46	19	35
01 (p. 23)	1965	Oregon College of Education	32	50	22	28
		Oregon State University	42	27	50	23
		University of Oregon	39	38	34	28
		Portland State College	17	48	28	24

*Because the authors compared faculty attitudes on questions having a somewhat different phrasing from study to study, we have combined the responses of the several studies as follows: Favorable (including any degree of favorableness); Unfavorable (including any degree of unfavorableness); and Neutral (including indifferent, undecided, don't know, and no response).

† Oregon State College became Oregon State University in 1961.

NOTE: The full citation to source is identified by study number in the *Bibliography* related to the special subject of this and each succeeding table.

SOURCE: Dubin & Hedley, 1969, p. 32.

TABLE 5
The personal
use of ETV
is viewed
with some
hesitancy

QUESTION: How would you like to try out closed-circuit television in one or more of your classes?*

Source-study number	Year of study	Academic institution	N	Attitude toward personally experimenting with ETV		
				Favor-able	Neutral	Unfavor-able
32	1955–56	Pennsylvania State University	177	43%	30%	27%
	1956–57		140	45	24	31
	1957–58		143	33	28	39
	1958–59		136	39	12	49
31 (pp. 340–341)	1957	State University of Iowa	160	51	10	39
28 (p. 50)	1957	Oregon College of Education	40	42	43	15
	1959		28	25	36	39
	1957	Oregon State College	256	28	51	21
	1959		171	23	47	30
	1957	University of Oregon	208	24	40	36
	1959		123	26	38	36
	1957	Willamette University	50	26	26	48
	1959		26	15	43	42
29 (p. 32)	1961	University of Minnesota	892	36	34	30

*See notes, Table 4.
SOURCE: Dubin & Hedley, 1969, p. 36.

members will come to institutions aware of the potentials of the expanding technology and less resistant to its teaching-learning applications. If, as we have recommended in Section 6 of this report, appropriate institutional encouragement and incentives are given, we believe more and more faculty members will become involved in the design and development of instructional materials that employ the new technologies. They could find their task in this regard facilitated by the emergence of new ranks of educational professionals who will assist them in their instruction-planning endeavors.

ROLES FOR
NEW PROFES-
SIONALS

As the variety of instructional alternatives for each lesson and course increases, the planning of instruction will require more differentiated knowledge and skills than most individual professors are likely to have. Ideally, the task could involve at least four specialists:

The teacher   He or she is the member of the team who best understands what needs to be taught. The teacher has prepared himself for his role by years of concentration on the subject from which course content is to be drawn. The teacher also understands the relationship of the course to others on related subjects and to the objectives of the students who elect to take it. The teacher knows which parts of a course are hard to grasp and which are easy—and best understands what lessons need to be emphasized.

We see no reason to alter the subject matter orientation of a faculty member's preparation. We cannot overemphasize, however, the importance of creating more opportunities for faculty members to learn the art of teaching through courses leading to Doctor of Arts degrees or other appropriate certification for college-level teaching. A part of that learning should be the acquisition of an understanding of the capabilities of various instructional media and practice in working with other specialists in the creation of instructional programs.

The instructional technologist   This member of the team is a specialist in the learning process. His or her job is to help faculty members define the objectives of courses of instruction, to plot the learning strategies to be employed, and to evaluate results. Where such specialists have been used in planning instruction elsewhere, and notably by Great Britain's Open University, they have often been accepted initially with considerable skepticism by faculty. Eventually, however, they have been regarded as absolutely essential to the task of planning instruction both with and without the new media.

Persons who have the expertise envisaged by our concept of the instructional technologist typically will have concentrated on educational psychology, behavioral psychology, or social psychology in preparation. We would expect them to have received educational preparation at least to master's level and preferably to the doctoral level.

The media technologist   This member of the team is the one who best understands the capabilities of available media. The media technologist should know how to organize the technological resources needed for effective instruction, should warn his colleagues away from media that are ineffective for contemplated tasks, and urge upon them only such technological power as is sufficient to the job at hand. The media technologist who participates in instructional development is much more than the one who holds the key to the equipment cabinet; this person may supervise others who maintain and operate instructional equipment, but his or her role in instructional dvelopment is a creative one.

There may be several paths of preparation for media technologists. On large campuses, with sophisticated media capabilities, the need may be for a variety of specialists that includes computer scientists, electronic engineers, television and radio technicians, editors, and film or television directors. It would be unreasonable to expect small campuses to have such a wide variety of specialists on their staffs, but they should have them available as needed on a consulting basis or through cooperative arrangements with other institutions. The educational preparation of these specialists will vary and obviously will involve concentration in the subjects of their specialization. Some of them will require doctorates, others will need only master's degrees or occupational degrees. All should have a combination of educational preparation and practical experience adequate to insure full collegiality among members of instructional planning teams.

The information specialist   The fourth member of the team is the one who guides his colleagues to information essential for the preparation of instructional materials. The reach of this specialist should go beyond the walls of the campus library and, for that matter, beyond the campus gates. It is his or her job to know wherever the needed data, illustrations, films, slides, audiotapes and other instructional "software" that might be used for a course are to be found. The information specialist therefore is in a pivotal position to affect the richness and quality of the instructional programs.

Educational preparation for this position should be undertaken either in a school of librarianship or in preparation for a master's degree in an academic subject. Research experience is essential.

In estimating the numbers of technologists and specialists needed in higher education, it should be kept in mind that they will not work together 100 percent of the time, and the full range of personnel will not be required for every course or project. Most of the time, the professor will be on his own—just as he always has been. In the course-planning stages the team will work together, but with different members of the team directly involved for varying lengths of time. After a course is planned, the professor will probably call upon team members only intermittently for consultation, evaluation, and assistance with course revision (which can be almost as time-consuming, using the new media, as course origination). It is reasonable to expect that the specialist members of an instructional planning team could work in a concentrated way with perhaps 10 professors in an academic year, and might reasonably be able to serve 50 faculty members over a five-year period. To serve more, the team would have to either increase the time lapse between full course reviews or compress the time allowed for assisting in the initial development of courses of instruction. To provide at least three specialists to assist every 50 professors will require employment of as many as 45,000 new instructional professionals in higher education by 1980 and 54,000 by 2000.[1] Large institutions may require more instructional professionals because of the broader range of subject matter offered. Community colleges, and some comprehensive colleges, may require a higher ratio of instructional professionals to faculty members, because of heavier course loads per instructor. We would urge, in the meantime, that some institutions of higher learning arrange now for the introduction of instruction designed to train the new specialists who will have new career opportunities in higher education in the coming decades. Universities and comprehensive colleges will have particularly significant responsibilities for training persons as instructional technologists, media technologists, and information specialists. Comprehensive colleges and community colleges will make important contributions in the training of certain categories of media specialists and large numbers of support technicians who will become involved in instructional technology at the production and operation level.

Recommendation 13: Colleges and universities should supplement their instructional staffs with qualified technologists and specialists

---

[1] In estimating these needs it is estimated that the average student-teacher ratio will be about 17 to 1 in 1980 and will increase by a factor of two additional students by the year 2000. We assume 12,500,000 students by 1980 and 16,000,000 students by the year 2000 (Carnegie Commission on Higher Education, 1971*b*). It should be noted that an unknown number of persons with the desired special qualifications of the professionals needed are already employed in various capacities on college and university campuses.

to assist instructors in the design, planning, and evaluation of teaching-learning units that can be used with the expanding instructional technologies. Institutions of higher education at all levels should develop their potentials for training specialists and professionals needed to perform the new functions that are associated with the increasing utilization of instructional technology on the nation's college and university campuses.

ROLES OF TEACHING ASSISTANTS Instructional technology will probably have off-setting effects on teaching assistants. To the degree that instructional technology permits more independent instruction, frees faculty members for closer student contact, and assumes a larger role in drill and testing, it should reduce the need for teaching assistants. On the other hand, the same trends may increase the need for teaching assistants as individual tutors to assist students having difficulty with self-instruction, and as proctors supervising the use of self-instruction equipment. In the latter role, they will be an important communication link between the students and faculty members, and will be able to report first-hand knowledge of the effectiveness of instructional media employed.

Because early involvement in the work of instructional development teams will be of value to teaching assistants as future college and university teachers, opportunities for such participation should be provided whenever it is feasible and appropriate to do so.

8. *Impacts on Students*

The new technology, as we have already noted, holds two major promises for students. The first is that they will become more active agents in their own education. The second is that they will have more flexibility and variety in their education.

Independent learning is inherent in such technologies as printed course "modules," dial-access audiovisual instruction, individualized learning laboratories, and the tutorial use of the computer. Although human tutors and instructors may supervise the use of such technologies and stand by for consultation and guidance, the students themselves initiate the learning experience and perform the learning chores required by whatever mode they are using. Their pride in learning sharpens as their responsibility for it is enlarged.

Although there have been many warnings about the "impersonality" of technologies used in instruction, that danger is present in any situation in which large numbers of students must be served by relatively smaller numbers of professors. And some institutions that make little use of instructional technologies may provide less opportunities for student-teacher contact than those that use it extensively. Moreover, we believe that David Riesman's observation cited in the Commission on Instructional Technology report bears repetition:

A machine is not a sadist and does not suffer from rebuffs or redundancy. Nor does a student feel demeaned by having to take instruction from a person of another class or race or sex. For a boy who feels that, like Huckleberry Finn, he must light out for the Territory to prove his manhood, or for a black student who feels that a white teacher is subjecting him to counterfeit nurturance and thus making him even weaker and more deprived, or for a lower-class white student who feels a similar uneasiness at being helped, the machine can be a marvelously neutral substitute.

Few teachers are sadists; they are, however, human and naturally react to the above reactions of students and to the constraints of conventional school organizations. The machine can spare both student and teacher (Tickton, 1970, p. 32).

The flexibility promised by instructional technology is poignantly summed up in a description of Physics 13 written for its students at Dartmouth by Prof. Arthur Luehrmann. In that brief mimeographed document, he indicated that the course is divided into study units; for each there is a study guide which, among other things:

> . . . lists *references* to places you can go to learn about the material in the unit. Usually there will be a reference to certain pages in your text book— Halliday and Resnick's *Physics*. There will also be references to other similar text books quite different from yours. There may also be a reference to a film loop that you can run on a projector in 220 Wilder or an Audio-Cassette mini-lecture or a video-tape lecture or demonstration. There may be a reference to a computer program in the Dartmouth Time-Sharing System. There may be a reference to the laboratory. Different students may have different styles of learning, and we want to offer many routes that lead to the objectives stated in the study guide (Luehrmann, n.d.).

Significantly, this document also advises the students that another physics course, "with more nearly equivalent content" than in previous years, would be taught in the conventional lecture mode simultaneously by another professor. "If . . . you decide that it [Physics 13] isn't for you, you may transfer to Physics 3 . . ." (ibid.).

There are other courses taught in much the same way elsewhere in the country but there are not many. As more of them become available, they may well counter some of the major dissatisfactions of American students today.

Educational technology is not the only answer to this dissatisfaction. Another very important answer, obviously, is for colleges and universities to increase their efforts to hire more teachers of outstanding ability. But that is not always a realistic option. Educational technology can make a contribution to the quality of instruction in several ways:

- It can give a student access to presentations by exceptionally talented and knowledgeable teachers who live and work at great distances from the student's campus.

- It can give a student access to instructional programs designed with bigger budgets, more expertise, and greater talent than can be found on a single campus.

- It can enrich and supplement classroom instruction that is already available.

- It can give a student alternative modes of instruction for the same subject.

Another source of dissatisfaction on the part of undergraduates, regardless of the types of institutions they attend, is the variety of courses offered. As educational technology continues to develop it should become feasible for any institution with basic learning resource facilities to offer instruction on any subject that has been taught effectively anywhere. What one college's faculty cannot teach, other teachers possibly can, and their instruction can be made widely available by using technology. The assurance that technology can fill such gaps depends only upon the speed with which instructional programs can be developed, and the ability of institutions to share successful instructional packages.

THE NEED FOR NEW STUDENT SKILLS At the present time, independent use of instructional media being introduced into colleges and universities makes no demands upon student skills that cannot be met with the help of a relatively simple briefing. Frequently, the most that is required is the flip of a switch or the mounting of cassettes or film reels for playback.

Even the use of computers for much of the instruction that is available today requires more typing skill than comprehension of computer programming. But this is subject to change. Some observers have noted that a great deal of time is now spent in schools teaching children how to do calculations that they will rarely if ever have to do in the future without the assistance of a computer. The conclusion to be drawn from such observations is not that we are being overwhelmed by technology or that we no longer need to teach mathematics. The useful conclusion is that the computer is going to have increasing impact on our everyday life. One implication of that conclusion is that young people ought to develop skills in communicating with computers as early as possible.

We are encouraged to note that some of the instructional components designed for computer use have built-in learning units that are designed to familiarize the student with the capacities and design of computers and the theories that underlie their programs.

We believe, however, that some computer skills should be learned even before a student enters college. The skill may prove educationally indispensable. And even if it does not, it is hard to conceive of its not being useful.

It is important that colleges begin now to train more prospective high school instructors in the use of computers. It is also important that more high schools introduce instruction in computer operation so that by the year 2000, when the new computer technologies are in general instructional use, entering college students will have been adequately trained for its use.

Recommendation 14: <u>High schools that do not already do so should offer instruction in basic concepts and uses of computers and should encourage their students to obtain, as early as possible, other skills that will be helpful in the use of new media for learning.</u>

In stressing the learning of computer skills at an early stage, we do not intend to imply that students should not have opportunities to gain expertise with other technologies. Both still photography and motion picture photography, for instance, are legitimate forms of expression and, for certain subject matter, are as valid for demonstrating learned insights as the essay or term paper. Exercises in the transfer of knowledge by whatever medium should be as much learning experiences as they are tests. Opportunities for students to develop skills in the creative use of any communications medium are therefore of considerable value. But it is doubtful that such skills will become as generally indispensable to learning as those relating to the computer.

INFORMING STUDENTS As different systems of learning are developed for the same courses, and as students need to know not only what instruction is available on their own campuses but also what is available by remote access through cooperative learning-technology centers or distant institutions, the problem of giving them adequate information and advice about available learning options becomes even more important than it is now. The need for personnel to assist students in making effective choices will become more urgent as instructional technologies are adopted, and the employment of such persons will be an added expense of introducing new media and instruction modes to a college campus that probably cannot be avoided.

To the degree that the new instructional technology makes it possible for students at many different institutions to receive the same learning programs, a question arises concerning which standards should be applied in measuring student performance and achievement. Should all students instructed by such learning units be examined by the same testing instruments, or should they be examined by instruments devised by their own institutions? If all students using a standard learning unit are tested by a standard test, students with average ability as measured nationally but with above-average ability when measured in the context of their own institution's average student-ability level could be unfairly penalized. Can centrally devised examinations properly reflect the instructional objectives of individual institutions? Should institutions abdicate responsibility for setting performance standards by accepting the standards of an outside agency?

Ideally, a faculty member selecting a centrally produced learning unit for use in his course will do so on the basis of the ability of that unit to serve learning objectives he himself has determined. It would follow that, to the greatest extent possible, the faculty member himself should devise the examinations that test the achievement and performance of the students that use the unit and assume responsibility for the standards maintained for students taking his course. If different institutions use standardized tests, instructors might use the results to gauge the performance of their students against a national or regional norm. But an instructor should not use such tests to rate students on their performance in meeting his own teaching objectives.

As the variety of teaching-learning modes available to students increases, there will be growing needs for tests designed to provide students with realistic assessments of their chances of learning success with specific media and programs. It is well known that different students learn different things best under different conditions. Developing ways to diagnose a student's most effective learning mode and environment may become crucial to the appropriate use of instructional technology and should become a top priority interest of persons and agencies engaged in the development and utilization of educational testing procedures.

Measuring performance and achievement in extramural instruction programs that rely heavily on technology and independent study is now a subject of considerable debate. What performance and achievements are to be measured? How will degrees based on such tests compare with degrees earned in traditional colleges and universities? Current research contributions of major testing services and other agencies interested in these matters are very welcome, and the results will be awaited with great interest.

9. Costs of Instructional Technology

It is certain that the costs of introducing more of the new technology into higher education are going to be high. Just how high they will be, however, is virtually impossible to estimate.

DIFFICULTIES IN COST ESTIMATION 1 There is not now any uniform pattern of technology utilization from institution to institution. Few institutions are using all the technology that is available, and in some of the uses—notably of computers—distinctions are not made between instructional and other applications. Even institutions that use the same basic media use it quite differently. On one campus, film is used straight from the can to the projector. On another it may be reprocessed and delivered via videotape to remote-access learning stations (and the computer that controls the transaction may be regarded as having no standing at all as an instructional medium).

2 There are considerable economic differences between the impact of the mere availability and the actual use of instructional technology by a campus. On a cost-per-student-hour measurement, a seldom-used moving picture production and projection facility may compare unfavorably with a fairly expensive computer facility that is heavily used.

3 Much of the available cost data for instructional technology is for elementary and secondary education. Although it is reasonable to assume that technology does not discriminate against age and that basic costs will remain the same regardless of the level at which technology is applied, the assumption has not been thoroughly tested. One almost certain difference is that salaries for personnel are likely to be lower in elementary and secondary education than they are in colleges and universities.

4   In efforts to standardize patterns of media utilization for purposes of comparison, writers on the subject of costs have been forced to employ hypothetical models with built-in assumptions that may not be realized in actual use. Examples include hypothetical community sizes or technology use in some arbitrarily assumed fraction of total instruction time. In the absence of solid cost data based on actual experience there is no alternative to this approach, but its deficiencies should be recognized by those who use the results in making policy.

5   Cost estimates often refer to a specific time and a fixed state of the arts in instructional technology. No allowances are made for decreases in certain costs as technology becomes more widely used.

6   The anticipated nature of institutional utilization of a given medium may be different from the actual use. It makes a great deal of difference, for instance, whether an institution using films acquires them from off-campus sources or makes its own (as some cost studies apparently contemplate).

7   There have been relatively few technologywide cost studies. Most studies involve only one medium, and compatability of one study with another is seldom possible.

Despite all these difficulties, we believe efforts must continue to be made to collect and analyze cost information on the use of technology for instruction in higher education. Such efforts could appropriately be made by the cooperative learning-technology centers whose establishment we have recommended in Section 6 of this report.

COSTS AND PRODUCTIVITY   For most institutions, expenditures for introducing the new instructional technologies onto their campuses will be in the form of add-on costs. In return for such expenditures they will not realize immediate savings. Instead, they will enrich the content of their instruction, obtain flexibility in scheduling classes, and generate variety in the instructional modes and opportunities made available to their students. They will also acquire capacity to increase their productivity.

Historically, costs of providing higher education in the United States have risen much faster than the number of students who receive it. As Baumol and Bowen point out (1966, p. 171) colleges and universities are in this respect like the performing arts; they provide little opportunity for systematic and cumulative increases in productivity. The performing artist's productivity—represented by the size of his audience—is restricted by the size of the hall in which he performs and the number of times he can repeat the same performance to different audiences. Similarly, in the conventional teaching mode, teachers are limited in their production by the size of their classes and the limited opportunities they have each year to repeat the same instruction. Performing artists increase their productivity through recordings, films, or performing on television. And the entertainment provided in these forms is available at a much smaller cost per viewer or listener than are live performances. College and university professors can use the new instructional technology to increase their productivity. Among the ways technology can help are the following:

By decreasing the time required by students to learn specified modules of information An example of this kind of savings is the Multi-Media Economic Analysis course devised by Sterling Institute for use at the U.S. Naval Academy. It compacted the normal instruction time from two semesters to one semester and 32 percent of the students completed the course before the end of the semester with a final grade of A or B (Furey, 1970, p. 4).

By taking maximum advantage of the capabilities of available technological capacity Dartmouth's 142 terminals for student and faculty use of its Time Sharing System for computing have reduced cost per student for the computing facility to $60 a year. Student and faculty use accounted for over 70 percent of the terminal services provided in 1970–71 (Kiewit Computation Center, 1971), and this high rate of utilization significantly reduced the cost per individual user.

By releasing faculty time By making use of media which result in considerable independent learning, teacher time for lecturing and class preparation can be reduced. Self-instruction laboratory units, such as those pioneered at Purdue University by S. W. Postlethwaite, can produce such savings. Typically the professor's lecture time is reduced by about two-thirds in courses taught in this mode. The savings may be to some extent offset by the costs of tutors who supervise the laboratory sessions, but at some institutions these costs might be no greater than the costs of teaching assistants needed for instruction in the traditional mode.

By prolonging the time during which instruction is available This saving, which can be realized by providing independent learning opportunities, removes the need for increasing personnel to double up on the instruction of the same course in order to accommodate additional students.

By utilizing quality instructional materials produced off the campus The obvious saving here is in the time required to prepare instruction. Another is in spreading the use of an instruction segment over a long period of time. At Oral Roberts University, the BBC series, "Civilisation," was cut into segments for student viewing on the institution's remote-access system as part of a cultural history course. Similar use was made of CBS's "Interviews with Lord North."

By sharing high-quality instructional programs and learning materials with other institutions As more good instructional materials become available, sharing should become more commonplace. It has the effect of reducing cost-of-course preparation on the campuses of both the originator and of the sharing institution.

By a conscientious integration of all available technologies to produce desired objectives This is cost efficiency at its highest level of sophistication. It need not utilize the more spectacular technologies at all. But it is hard to achieve. One example is found at Oklahoma Christian College, an institution that is best known in instructional technology circles for its learning center featuring carrels for each of its more than 1,200 students and the availability of some 136 instruction segments through a dial-access audio system. While the effectiveness of this system as a use of audio-recording devices is questioned by some technologists, the college's meticulous concern for the utilization of relatively modest instructional media and the effective organization of instructional space has resulted in a good record of productivity per faculty member of some 827.3 student credit hours. This was some 250 hours more than the highest ranking institution among 13 liberal arts colleges compared in a recent study by the Council for the Advancement of Small Colleges.

By enlarging the market for instructional materials and instructional media As long as instructional technology remains experimental and is used sporadically on the nation's campuses, the marketplace for instructional materials will remain constricted; enthusiasm for developing such materials will be dampened; and cost of savings that would follow an active commerce in instructional materials will be denied to higher education.

We believe, however, that the initial decision to utilize instructional technology should be based at least as much on educational objectives as it is on costs. In this respect, we find the advice of C. R. Carpenter (1968, p. 9) worth repeating:

There are possibilities for misuse of every expensive and complex communication aparatus. Some examples are found in the employment of TV broadcasting stations on the regional or national network scale for the instruction of a relatively small number of individuals. Similarly, closed-circuit TV systems, radio facilities, and computers may be committed to teaching tasks for which they are not appropriate or which use only a fraction of the available information-processing capacity of the equipment. In general, it may be said that mass media are better not used with small groups or for limited individual instruction, except in experimental or research applications.

A general prescription for avoiding serious misuse of instructional facilities has two parts: The materials and equipment should be designed, selected, and used to serve specific functions of teaching and to provide the best possible conditions for learning. Second, there should be a close matching of capacities of the technology with instructional requirements. Furthermore, regardless of fashions and fads in educational facilities the simplest and most economical equipment that will perform well the defined and required instructional functions should be employed. In brief, solving the problem of determining the most appropriate uses for equipment requires the best matching of functions and capacities with the demands of instructional tasks.

In the Commission's forthcoming report, *The More Effective Use of Resources: An Imperative for Higher Education,* we will recommend steps that can be taken by colleges and universities to produce savings, some of which might appropriately be applied to meet the expenses of expanding the use of the new teaching and learning technologies on their campuses. Also, in an earlier section of this report we recommended the establishment of cooperative learning-technology centers. One of their central functions would be to provide institutions with ways to share costs and resources so that even the most expensive of the new instructional media can be made available to individual colleges that could not afford them on their own. These measures should help institutions meet the add-on costs of instructional technology that will be required in the short-run.

Perhaps as early as the mid-1980s, these expenditures could begin to yield increasing productivity in the form of more students taught per hour invested in instruction. By that time, if our recommendations are accepted and a concerted effort has been made to advance instructional technology, more instructional materials will be available and will be more intensively used for longer periods of time than they are now. Costs of some of the instructional hardware will begin to go down as it becomes more standardized and is produced in larger quantities than it is now. Investments in the materials and media themselves will therefore become more productive.

Still greater productivity will occur in the saving of time spent in instruction by faculty members. Those faculty members who actively engage in the development of widely used instructional materials will reach more students over longer periods of time with any one instructional unit produced through their efforts. With the use of technology more students can learn in independent modes that save faculty time for teaching additional courses or more students. Student-faculty ratios can therefore increase without inevitable loss of quality in instruction. Such increases will occur on the campuses themselves. But they will be most spectacularly observed in the ratio of all students engaged in higher learning to all professors and instructional professionals so involved when the full impacts of many thousands of new students enrolled in technology–intensive extramural higher education is felt.

THE NEED FOR INDEPENDENT ASSESSMENT We are confident that the expanding instructional technology will improve learning, make learning and teaching more challenging to students and teachers alike, and yield cost savings as it becomes more widely used and reduces the need for live instruction. It may, indeed, provide the best means available to us for solving the difficult problem of continuing to educate growing numbers of students of all ages within a budget the American people can afford.

But enthusiasm should be balanced by caution. We have only begun to glimpse the potentials of instructional technology and have only begun to give serious attention to its advancement. At least for the coming three decades we believe that our efforts to utilize and improve the new instructional technology should be accompanied by periodic review of progress and results.

Recommendation 15: An independent commission, supported either by an appropriate agency of the United States Department of Health, Education and Welfare or by one or more private foundations should be created to make assessments of the instructional effectiveness and cost benefits of currently available instructional technology. Findings of the commission should be published and appropriately disseminated for the advice of institutions of higher education, such cooperative learning-technology centers as may be established, and governments and foundations supporting the advancement of instructional technology.

10. Reasonable Goals for Instructional Technology

Although the advocates of instructional technology accept the importance of objectives for the learning process, they have been negligent in defining reasonable objectives for the development of technology itself. They have, instead, stressed potentials of the new media and systems, sometimes overstating the case and thus creating fears among those who value the security of the status quo, and fixing disbelief in the minds of those who appreciate the difficulties with which fundamental changes can be accomplished. We prefer a goals approach that concentrates attention on what is both possible and needed.

BY 1980   The Carnegie Commission suggests that the following goals be reached by 1980.

1   *Institutions of higher learning will have accepted a broad definition of instructional technology such as: The enrichment and improvement of the conditions in which human beings learn and teach achieved through the creative and systematic organization of resources, physical arrangements, media, and methods.*

Acceptance of a broad definition of instructional technology is not a matter of semantic convention. It is a tactical step that is necessary to assure that technology will be regarded as subservient to the needs of teaching and learning and not an end in itself. It is also necessary because it conceives of the various media and technologies as working in conjunction with one another, and combines the support and enthusiasm now given to diverse individual technologies into efforts on behalf of the general development of teaching and learning resources. Finally, it embraces technologies whose merits have been established by many years of use, as well as the novel ones that have been only recently introduced.

2 *Most colleges and universities will have devised adequate administrative and academic authority and procedures for the encouragement and appropriate utilization of instructional technology.*

Although many segments of our society have roles to play in the development of instructional technology, educational institutions have the greatest stake in its utilization. Until they exert some leadership in the design and application of learning materials and some demand for effective media, it is unlikely that governments will be able to advance the cause of technology through additional financial support alone or that industry can advance it solely through dedication of production and distribution capabilities for instructional hardware and software. If the development and use of instructional technology on the campuses is made the explicit responsibility of the principal academic officers of institutions, a significant first-step will have been taken.

3 *Colleges and universities who are responsible for training prospective teachers for high schools and colleges will have incorporated instruction in the design of courses and in the effective utilization of instructional technology (as broadly defined in this report) in their curricula.*

The increasing use of technology in instruction will require the availability of teachers who understand the capabilities and limitations of new and expanding media and the procedures involved in effective course design. Preparation of such teachers should not be delayed, because even students who are now preparing to be teachers and professors will be teaching in the year 2000 when we expect instructional technology to be in general use.

4 *A concerted federal government effort, utilizing the resources of the nation's finest libraries and museums as well as the resources of the nation's campuses, will have been made to design and produce courses of instruction of good quality for presentation using advanced electronic media.*

The greatest deficiency in instructional technology at the present time is caused by the inadequate supply of teaching and learning materials of good quality suitable for use with the new technologies. We have recommended that colleges and universities encourage the development of such materials on their own campuses. Beyond the campuses, instructional programs must be developed for utilization by many different institutions in the form of films, video- and audiocassettes, or printed learning modules. Because such forms are least expensive and most effective when widely used, it is especially important they be expertly prepared, drawing upon the best available expertise and learning resources. We therefore believe that resource centers such as the Smithsonian Institution, National Gallery of Art, the Library of Congress, the National Archives, and major metropolitan cultural centers should be used to sponsor and assist in the development of high-quality instructional materials suitable for presentation with various media.

5 *At least three cooperative learning-technology centers, combining the instructional technology capabilities of many member institutions within a geographic region, and originating and directing centralized instructional services through information, communications, and computing networks will be in operation.*

A critical need in instructional technology is for organized effort to create, improve, and utilize effective instructional programs that can take advantage of existing media and know-how. Such efforts require a focus and level of expenditures that cannot be provided by individual institutions.

Through the combined efforts of cooperative learning-technology centers and the institutions described in (4) above, at least 500 instructional units ranging from course-length to quarter-hour segments, all suitable for use with media in their contemporary state of development, could be made nationally available by 1975. As many as 1,500 units could be available by 1980.

6 *The level of federal support for development and application of instructional technologies should have reached a figure equal to 1 percent of the total national expenditure for higher education.*

Individual institutions should contribute as much funding as they possibly can to efforts to advance instructional technology. In view of current financial stringencies faced by many colleges and universities, however, it is now impossible for them to make the full investments that are needed. The federal government must therefore continue to play a major role in supporting instructional technology developments until at least the end of the current century. We have recommended that by 1980 such support should equal 1 percent of the annual national expenditures on higher education.

7 *Extramural higher education programs should be available to most Americans through Open University type programs initiated by existing colleges and universities, states, or cooperative learning-technology centers.*

These new programs will provide for some people an alternative to traditional higher education. But they will also be able to serve — and undoubtedly will attract — many thousands of learners who are not counted in the normal estimates for conventional colleges and universities. These additional thousands of learners can only be served if an adequate instructional technology exists to supplement the services of live faculty members available for such programs, and to accommodate learning that traverses great distances and schedules of students for whom education is not a primary activity. The very existence of such systems should stimulate the development of instructional technology generally.

8 *Legal restraints upon the duplication of educational materials should have been thoroughly reviewed by Congress with special attention given to their impacts on the capabilities and advantages of instruction provided by the new instructional technology.*

9 *Manufacturers of equipment for uses in teaching and learning at colleges and universities will have made a greater effort to adapt their designs so that compatible instructional components can be produced for use on a wide variety of makes and models.*

The lack of standardization and compatibility in much of the mediaware that can be used for instruction in higher education impairs the full and early development of educational technology. Some standardization will inevitably occur, as it has in other media, under pressures of the marketplace. But we would also encourage government agencies and manufacturers' associations to influence, to the extent they are able, a more rapid accommodation by information and communications industries to instructional needs for a wide variety of materials that are usable on a broad range of available equipment models. The needs are particularly acute in the use of media that utilize computer programs, audio-tapes, and videocassettes.

10 *Systems for identifying promising instructional materials will have been developed, and procedures for encouraging their development and utilization will be operable.*

11 *New professions for persons engaged in creating and developing instructional materials on the nation's campuses will have emerged.*

BY 1990   **1** *Most colleges in the country will have introduced sufficient technologies of all available and appropriate kinds to realize the following benefits:*

(a) Savings of some of the time professors and senior instructors traditionally spend in personally presenting information that could as easily be presented by other means. A reasonable goal is average savings of at least 15 percent of a professor's time per course.

(b) Provision of alternative modes of instruction for existing courses. There is no longer any reason to insist that students learn everything in the same way. Some students learn some things best from the lecture mode. Others learn certain things best by reading or with maximum use of visual materials. Particularly in fact-intensive courses, or review courses that are prerequisites for advanced instruction, students should have as wide a variety of learning modes available as possible.

(c) Provision of logistical flexibility by allowing students to receive certain amounts of their instruction at times and places that are most convenient to them.

2 *Six of the seven proposed cooperative learning-technology centers recommended in Section 6 will be in operation.*

BY 2000   **1** *All instructional technology identifiable in 1972 will be in general use on college and university campuses.*

2 *The availability of education through independent study within and without traditional institutions will have become widespread through applications of the expanding technology.*

The year 2000 could also mark the completion of more than 25 years of concentrated effort toward the advancement of learning through instructional technology. At this point it should be feasible for teachers and students to contemplate the ultimate dream of all those who have given serious thought to the potentials of the new media — a national interconnection of independent information, communication, and instructional resources, with the combined capacity of making available to any student, anywhere in the country, at any time, learning from the total range of accumulated human knowledge.

Appendix : Some Observations on Costs

From assorted sources, it is possible to derive cost estimates for various forms of instructional technology, but such estimates must be regarded only as examples. They often apply to specific applications of particular models of equipment used for student groups of specific sizes. Different combinations of equipment and applications would result in different costs.

One particularly useful source of cost information is Appendix C to the report of the Commission on Instructional Technology. In that report (Tickton, 1970, pp. 84–85) the following examples were cited:

- About $700 can buy a 16-mm film projector.

- Fifty to sixty thousand dollars can cover the initial cost of a dial-access information system in a college or university, but costs can run into the hundreds of thousands of dollars.

- On the average, a closed-circuit television system costs $178,000 to install and can be operated for $86,000 a year.

- Nine self-instructional units of a physiology course developed and produced at Michigan State University, making use of carrels, audio tapes, slides, 8-mm films, and programmed texts, cost $40,000.

- The high school physics course produced by the Physical Sciences Study Committee (PSSC) cost $6.5 million.

- The Midwest Program on Airborne Television Instruction cost $18 million for the period 1961–1965.

- A simple television lecture can be produced for as little as $50 an hour, while the presentation making use of film and other visual materials might cost as much as $6,000 an hour.

A few other selected samples of costs:

- It is estimated that the first year's programs for "Sesame Street" were produced at a cost of $6.5 million (Grayson, 1972, p. 1221).

- Great Britain's Open University spent approximately $3 million for the preparation of 300 courses offered in its first year. The instructional program relied heavily on special texts, television (30 percent), and radio (30 percent).

- During 1970–71, the United States Naval Academy at Annapolis installed an exact duplicate of the Darmouth Time-sharing System at an estimated cost of $2.2 million.

- F. C. Johnson and J. E. Dietrich (Tickton, 1971, **11**, p. 973) estimate the cost of one hour's broadcast television production to be $3,859.

In a report for the Carnegie Commission prepared under the direction of Roger E. Levien, George Comstock provided estimates of computer costs based on a 1967 survey of the Southern Regional Education Board. Projected expenditures per student on instructional computer use for 1971–72 estimated on the basis of that survey are presented in Appendix Table 1.

It should be kept in mind, however, that most of the instructional computer utilization reported in this study was in the character of instruction *about* the computer, or as a computational facility for other subjects, notably mathematics. Instructional use of computers in the tutorial or simulation mode accounted for very low percentages of total computer use.

In an analysis of educational technology, James G. Miller (1971) has prepared a table summarizing several important parameters for various instructional media (Table 2). The terms which describe the media in the table make clear what they are, with perhaps one or two exceptions. "On-line computer aids to learning and scholarship" refers to such technologies as Project MAC at MIT. An individual user of Project MAC can get access, by a remote terminal on-line to a large time-sharing computer, to a wide range of materials that can help him solve mathematical, scientific, and engineering problems; routines for displaying the results of such problem solutions; tests of students' content knowledge in different fields; psychological and behavioral tests; and references or abstracts of articles relevant to many academic tasks. All these materials are almost instantaneously available for the user to inter-

Degree level and enrollment	Projected average expenditure (in actual dollars)		Number of institutions	
	Public	Private	Public	Private
Associate				
Below 500	36	16	100	187
500–2,499	38	3	256	87
2,500–9,999	19	*	116	4
10,000–19,999	25	†	23	†
Over 20,000	†	†	†	†
Bachelor's				
Below 500	19	3	10	8
500–2,499	16	11	65	112
2,500–9,999	22	8	24	15
10,000–19,999	*	25	1	1
Over 20,000	†	†	†	†
Master's				
Below 500	*	25	4	97
500–2,499	8	27	40	156
2,500–9,999	16	22	133	58
10,000–19,999	14	19	8	2
Over 20,000	14	†	10	†
Doctorate				
Below 500	5	19	4	11
500–2,499	99	85	29	61
2,500–9,999	33	82	43	94
10,000–19,999	30	55	17	100
Over 20,000	36	16	6	100

TABLE 1 Projected expenditures per student on instructional computer use for 1971–72 (based on 1966–67 data and growth rate for all computer activity in higher education between 1966–67 and 1967–68)

*Data unavailable.
† No schools in category.
SOURCE: Levien, 1972, in press.

act within a "conversational" mode that requires little or no understanding of mathematics or computer programming.

The final medium in Appendix Table 2, "Other standard audiovisual aids," represents several different items including wall charts, physical models of any kind, such as crystals or parts of the body or machines or houses or mountains, microscope slide projectors, ordinary slide projectors, overhead projectors, moving picture projectors, and so forth.

TABLE 2 *Characteristics and costs of various instructional media (1969)*

Instructional medium	Can user carry it around?	Can user use it individually at school or college?	Can user use it individually at home?	Can user determine when it is to be used?
1. Class lecture	No	No	No	No
2. Small discussion group	No	No	No	No
3. Books and journals	Yes	Yes	Yes	Yes, unless another user has it
4. Printed programmed instruction	Yes	Yes	Yes	Yes
5. Computerized programmed instruction	No	Yes	Rarely	Yes, unless number of terminals is limited
6. On-line computer aids to learning and scholarship	No	Yes	Rarely	Yes, unless number of terminals is limited
7. Closed-circuit lectures on public address system	No	No	No	No
8. Educational radio	No	Yes	Yes	No
9. Dial-access audio tape recordings	No	Yes	Rarely	Yes
10. Broadcast live instructional TV	No	Yes	Sometimes	No
11. Closed-circuit live instructional TV	No	Yes	No	No
12. Broadcast tape-recorded instructional TV	No	Yes	Sometimes	No
13. Closed-circuit tape recorded instructional TV	No	Yes	No	No
14. Dial-access instructional TV	No	Yes	No	Yes, unless number of terminals is limited

Can user control rate of information flow and repeat if not understood?	Can user interact actively with input?	Is individualized "branching" possible?	Senses used	Can signals be sent on electronic network?	Costs (dollar per hour of use)
Rarely	No	No	Vision and Audition	No	0.15–3
Sometimes	Yes	Rarely	Vision and Audition	No	0.50–15
Yes	No	No	Vision	No	0.05–10
Yes	No	Yes	Vision	No	0.05–10
Yes	Yes	Yes	Vision and Audition	Yes	2–25
Yes	Yes	Yes	Vision	Yes	5–100
No	No	No	Audition	Yes	0.02–2
No	No	No	Audition	Yes	0.01–1
In same systems	Rarely	No	Audition	Yes	0.01–2
No	No*	No	Vision and Audition	Yes	0.02–10
No	No*	No	Vision and Audition	Yes	0.03–3
No*	No*	No	Vision and Audition	Yes	0.01–5
No*	No*	No	Vision and Audition	Yes	0.03–2
Sometimes	Rarely	No	Vision and Audition	Yes	0.50–5

TABLE 2 *(continued)*

Instructional medium	Can user carry it around?	Can user use it individually at school or college?	Can user use it individually at home?	Can user determine when it is to be used?
15. *Facsimile transmission of documents by electronic circuits*	Terminals can be portable and attached to any telephone	Yes	Possibly	Yes, during hours sender is able to transmit to user
16. *Automated storage and retrieval of written and graphic materials*	No	Yes	Rarely	Yes
17. *Other standard audiovisual aids*	Usually	Yes	Often	Yes

* Recent technological developments may remove these limitations in the future.
SOURCE: Miller, 1971, pp. 1012–1013.

The first two instructional media listed in Table 2 are the traditional media of education and do not require any artifacts beyond the instructor and the student. Furthermore, if one looks across the columns on the chart, it is apparent that no one medium has exactly the same characteristics as any of the others. To determine which media would be most effective in any given learning situation, it is necessary to know what constitutes an optimum learning environment. Research on learning and educational psychology clearly indicates that the optimum learning environment differs from individual to individual, from time to time, and for different educational goals. Nevertheless, Miller (ibid.) proposes that aids to learning are most useful if the student can

(a) carry them around, for then they are available whenever needed; (b) use them individually rather than having to coordinate his activities with class groups or other students; (c) use the aids anywhere, both at school or college and at home; (d) determine in terms of his own needs and schedule when to use the materials; (e) control the rate of flow of information inputs and outputs in the learning process, and repeat inputs at will if they are not understood; (f) interact actively with the aids, since active learning is generally recognized as being better than passive; (g) be able to have outputs from him influence the next input coming to him. This "branching" arrangement assures that, if he knows one fact in the progression of the

Can user control rate of information flow and repeat if not understood?	Can user interact actively with input?	Is individualized "branching" possible?	Senses used	Can signals be sent on electronic network?	Costs (dollar per hour of use)
No	No	No	Vision	Yes	2–15
Yes	Sometimes	Yes	Vision	Yes	2–100
Yes	Sometimes	Rarely	Vision and Audition	No	0.05–8

learning process, he is not given special training on it but goes on to the next one and so forth until he comes to a fact which he does not know or a problem which he cannot solve properly, after which he is given special training on that, his time being used for practice only on those facts or problems which he does not understand; *(h)* receive inputs in more than one sensory modality, since multiple sensory modalities represent multiple channels of input which reinforce each other. Learning aids are more useful if they can be transmitted over electronic networks so that they can reach the student at any place he happens to be, coming rapidly and accurately from any other geographical location. It is also desirable for their costs to be minimal in dollars per user hour, as well as in the time they consume of the student or instructor involved.

The last column of Table 2 includes both estimated operating costs and an appropriate portion of capital construction costs. For all the media there is a wide range in costs, because it is extraordinarily difficult to make even rough cost estimates with our present knowledge of media. Among the many variables which influence the dollar cost per user hour of these different media are: the number of students using the media at a given location and at a given time, the ratio between the number of students and the number of instructors, the amount of hardware employed in the particular system under study, the number of hours the hardware is used on the average by each student, the original costs of the hardware (which have been rapidly decreasing), whether the hardware is bought in large quantities, and whether the software needs to be written for the local system or has already been prepared for another system.

References

Allen, William H., and Don H. Coombs: *Trends in Instructional Technology, The ERIC at Stanford 1970 Planning Report,* Stanford, Calif., 1970.

Ashby, Eric: "Machines, Understanding, and Learning: Reflections on Technology in Education," *The Graduate Journal,* vol. 7, no. 2, Austin, Tex., 1967.

Baumol, William J., and William G. Bowen: *Performing Arts: The Economic Dilemma,* The Twentieth Century Fund, New York, 1966.

Becker, Joseph (ed.): *Interlibrary Communications and Information Networks,* American Library Association, Chicago, 1971.

Belzer, Jack: "Patterns of Development of Education in Information Science," in Sidney G. Tickson (ed.), *To Improve Learning,* R. R. Bowker Company, New York, 1970.

Bitzer, D. L., and D. Skaperdas: "The Design of an Economically Viable Large-scale Computer-based Education System," Computer-based Education Research Laboratory, University of Illinois, 1969, reprinted in R. E. Levien (ed.), *Computers in Instruction,* R-718-NSF/CCOM/RC, The Rand Corporation, Santa Monica, Calif., July 1971, pp. 14–33.

Bowen, Howard R., and Gordon K. Douglass: *Efficiency in Liberal Education: A Study of Comparative Instructional Costs for Different Ways of Organizing Teaching-Learning in a Liberal Arts College,* McGraw-Hill Book Company, New York, 1971.

Breitenfeld, Frederick, Jr.: "Instructional Television: The State of the Art," in Sidney G. Tickton (ed.), *To Improve Learning: An Evaluation of Instructional Technology,* vol. 1, R. R. Bowker Company, New York, 1970, pp. 137–160.

Brown, J. W., and J. W. Thornton, Jr.: *New Media in Higher Education,* National Education Association, Washington, D.C., 1963.

Burns, Judith: "The Joint Standards: Media or Mediocrity?," *Educational Technology,* September 1971, pp. 53–56.

103

Carnegie Commission on Educational Television: *Public Television: A Program for Action,* Bantam, New York, 1967.

Carnegie Commission on Higher Education: *Quality and Equality: New Levels of Federal Responsibility for Higher Education,* McGraw-Hill Book Company, New York, 1968.

Carnegie Commission on Higher Education: *Less Time, More Options: Education Beyond the High School,* McGraw-Hill Book Company, New York, 1971a.

Carnegie Commission on Higher Education: *New Students and New Places: Policies for the Future Growth and Development of American Higher Education,* McGraw-Hill Book Company, New York, 1971b.

Carpenter, C. Ray: "Instructional Functions of New Media," In J. W. Thornton, Jr., and J. W. Brown (eds.), *New Media and College Teaching,* Department of Audiovisual Instruction, National Education Association, Washington, D.C., 1968, pp. 3–14.

Centre for Educational Research and Innovation (CERI): *Educational Technology; The Design and Implementation of Learning Systems,* Organization for Economic Cooperation and Development, Paris, 1971.

Chu, Godwin C., and Wilber Schramm: *Learning from Television: What the Research Says,* Institute for Communication Research, Stanford, Calif., 1967.

Comstock, G. A.: "The Computer and Higher Education in California," in Roger Levien, *The Emerging Technology: Instructional Uses of the Computer in Higher Education,* to be published by McGraw-Hill Book Company, New York, 1972.

Cox, Kenneth A.: "Federal Telecommunications Policy and Library Information Networks," in Joseph Becker (ed.), *Interlibrary Communications and Information Networks,* American Library Association, Chicago, 1971.

Department of Audiovisual Instruction: *A Survey of Instructional Closed-Circuit Television 1967,* National Education Association, Washington, D.C., 1967.

Dubin, Robert, and R. Alan Hedley: *The Medium May be Related to the Message,* Center for the Advanced Study of Educational Administration, Eugene, Oreg., 1969.

Eurich, Alvin C.: *Reforming American Education: The Innovative Approach to Improving Our Schools and Colleges,* Harper & Row, New York, 1969.

Forsythe, Richard O.: "Instructional Radio: A Position Paper," Educational Resources Information Center (ERIC) at Stanford, Calif., December 1970, 15 pp. (Mimeographed.)

Furey, Mary Z.: *Multi-media Economic Analysis Project: Final Evaluation Report,* U.S. Department of Health, Education and Welfare, Educational Resources Information Center (ERIC), Washington, D.C., August 1970.

The German Tribune, no. 520, March 30, 1972, p. 12.

Grayson, Laurence P.: "Costs, Benefits, Effectiveness: Challenge to Educational Technology," *Science,* vol. 175, no. 4027, March 17, 1972.

Kiewit Computation Center: *Biennial Report, 1969–1971,* Hanover, N.H., 1971.

Komoski, P. Kenneth: "Toward the Development of Effective Instructional Technology for American Education," in Sidney G. Tickton (ed.), *To Improve Learning,* vol. 1, R. R. Bowker, New York, 1970.

Levien, Roger E.: *The Emerging Technology: Instructional Uses of the Computer in Higher Education,* to be published by McGraw-Hill Book Company, New York, 1972.

Luehrmann, Arthur: "About Physics 13 and the Keller Plan," Dartmouth College, n.d., 9 pp. (Mimeographed.)

Miller, James G.: "Deciding Whether and How to Use Educational Technology in the Light of Cost-effectiveness Evaluation," in Sidney G. Tickton (ed.), *To Improve Learning: An Evaluation of Instructional Technology,* vol. 2, R. R. Bowker Company, New York, 1971, pp. 1007–1027.

Molnar, A. R.: *Education Broadcasting Review,* vol. 3, 1969.

National Center for Educational Statistics: *Library Statistics of Colleges and Universities,* Fall 1969 Analytic Report, Washington, D.C., 1971.

Oettinger, Anthony: "Will Information Technologies Help Learning?," unpublished manuscript to appear in a forthcoming Carnegie Commission book to be edited by Carl Kaysen.

Saettler, Paul: *A History of Instructional Technology,* McGraw-Hill Book Company, New York, 1968.

The Sloan Commission on Cable Communications: *On the Cable: The Television of Abundance,* McGraw-Hill Book Company, New York, 1971.

Stetten, Kenneth J.: "The Technology of Small, Local Facilities for Instructional Use," in R. E. Levien (ed.), *Computers in Instruction,* R-718-NSF/CCOM/RC, The Rand Corporation, Santa Monica, Calif., July 1971, pp. 35–41.

Television and Radio in Swedish Education, Report of the Committee for Television and Radio in Education, Stockholm, n.d. (Mimeographed.)

Thornton, James W., Jr., and James W. Brown: *New Media in Higher Education,* National Education Association, Washington, D.C., 1967.

Thornton, James W., Jr., and James W. Brown (eds.): *New Media and College Teaching,* Department of Audiovisual Instruction, National Education Association, Washington, D.C., 1968.

Tickton, Sidney G. (ed.): *To Improve Learning: An Evaluation of Instructional Technology,* 2 vols., R. R. Bowker, New York, 1970 and 1971.

University of the Air in Japan, Report by The Preparatory Study Committee for the University of the Air, 1970, 20 pp.

Walsh, John: "The Open University: Breakthrough for Britain," *Science,* vol. 174, no. 4010, November 12, 1971.

Wilcox, Jarrod: "A Survey Forecast of New Technology in Universities and Colleges," working paper, Alfred P. Sloan School of Management, M.I.T., 1972.

Zannetos, Zenon D., and Michael Scott-Morton: *Efforts Toward an Associative Learning Instructional System,* Alfred P. Sloan School of Management, M.I.T., 1968.

Carnegie Commission on Higher Education

Sponsored Research Studies

BRIDGES TO UNDERSTANDING:
INTERNATIONAL PROGRAMS OF AMERICAN
COLLEGES AND UNIVERSITIES
Irwin T. Sanders and Jennifer C. Ward

GRADUATE AND PROFESSIONAL EDUCATION
1980:
A SURVEY OF INSTITUTIONAL PLANS
Lewis B. Mayhew

THE AMERICAN COLLEGE AND AMERICAN
CULTURE:
SOCIALIZATION AS A FUNCTION OF HIGHER
EDUCATION
Oscar and Mary F. Handlin

RECENT ALUMNI AND HIGHER EDUCATION:
A SURVEY OF COLLEGE GRADUATES
Joe L. Spaeth and Andrew M. Greeley

CHANGE IN EDUCATIONAL POLICY:
SELF-STUDIES IN SELECTED COLLEGES AND
UNIVERSITIES
Dwight R. Ladd

STATE OFFICIALS AND HIGHER EDUCATION:
A SURVEY OF THE OPINIONS AND
EXPECTATIONS OF POLICY MAKERS IN NINE
STATES
Heinz Eulau and Harold Quinley

ACADEMIC DEGREE STRUCTURES:
INNOVATIVE APPROACHES
PRINCIPLES OF REFORM IN DEGREE
STRUCTURES IN THE UNITED STATES
Stephen H. Spurr

COLLEGES OF THE FORGOTTEN AMERICANS:
A PROFILE OF STATE COLLEGES AND
REGIONAL UNIVERSITIES
E. Alden Dunham

FROM BACKWATER TO MAINSTREAM:
A PROFILE OF CATHOLIC HIGHER
EDUCATION
Andrew M. Greeley

THE ECONOMICS OF THE MAJOR PRIVATE
UNIVERSITIES
William G. Bowen
(Out of print, but available from University Microfilm

THE FINANCE OF HIGHER EDUCATION
Howard R. Bowen
(Out of print, but available from University Microfilm

ALTERNATIVE METHODS OF FEDERAL
FUNDING FOR HIGHER EDUCATION
Ron Wolk

INVENTORY OF CURRENT RESEARCH ON
HIGHER EDUCATION 1968
Dale M. Heckman and Warren Bryan Martin

*The following technical reports are available from the Carnegie Commission on Higher Education, 1947
Center Street, Berkeley, California 94704.*

RESOURCE USE IN HIGHER EDUCATION:
TRENDS IN OUTPUT AND INPUTS, 1930–1967
June O'Neill

TRENDS AND PROJECTIONS OF PHYSICIANS
IN THE UNITED STATES 1967–2002
Mark S. Blumberg

MENTAL ABILITY AND HIGHER EDUCATIONAL
ATTAINMENT IN THE 20TH CENTURY
Paul Taubman and Terence Wales

SOURCES OF FUNDS TO COLLEGES AND
UNIVERSITIES
June O'Neill

MAY 1970:
THE CAMPUS AFTERMATH OF CAMBODIA
AND KENT STATE
Richard E. Peterson and John A. Bilorusky

*The following reprints are available from the Carnegie Commission on Higher Education, 1947 Center
Street, Berkeley, California 94704.*

ACCELERATED PROGRAMS OF MEDICAL EDUCATION, *by Mark S. Blumberg, reprinted from*
JOURNAL OF MEDICAL EDUCATION, *vol. 46, no. 8, August 1971.*

SCIENTIFIC MANPOWER FOR 1970–1985, *by Allan M. Cartter, reprinted from* SCIENCE, *vol. 172, no. 3979, pp. 132–140, April 9, 1971.*

A NEW METHOD OF MEASURING STATES' HIGHER EDUCATION BURDEN, *by Neil Timm, reprinted from* THE JOURNAL OF HIGHER EDUCATION, *vol. 42, no. 1, pp. 27–33, January 1971.*

REGENT WATCHING, *by Earl F. Cheit, reprinted from* AGB REPORTS, *vol. 13, no. 6, pp. 4–13, March 1971.**

COLLEGE GENERATIONS—FROM THE 1930s TO THE 1960s, *by Seymour M. Lipset and Everett C. Ladd, Jr., reprinted from* THE PUBLIC INTEREST, *no. 25, Summer 1971.*

AMERICAN SOCIAL SCIENTISTS AND THE GROWTH OF CAMPUS POLITICAL ACTIVISM IN THE 1960s, *by Everett C. Ladd, Jr., and Seymour M. Lipset, reprinted from* SOCIAL SCIENCES INFORMATION, *vol. 10, no. 2, April 1971.*

THE POLITICS OF AMERICAN POLITICAL SCIENTISTS, *by Everett C. Ladd, Jr., and Seymour M. Lipset, reprinted from* PS, *vol. 4, no. 2, Spring 1971.**

THE DIVIDED PROFESSORIATE, *by Seymour M. Lipset and Everett C. Ladd, Jr., reprinted from* CHANGE, *vol. 3, no. 3, pp. 54–60, May 1971.*

JEWISH AND GENTILE ACADEMICS IN THE UNITED STATES: ACHIEVEMENTS, CULTURE AND POLITICS, *by Seymour M. Lipset and Everett C. Ladd, Jr., reprinted from* AMERICAN JEWISH YEAR BOOK, *1971.*

THE UNHOLY ALLIANCE AGAINST THE CAMPUS, *by Kenneth Keniston and Michael Lerner, reprinted from* NEW YORK TIMES MAGAZINE, *November 8, 1970 .*

PRECARIOUS PROFESSORS: NEW PATTERNS OF REPRESENTATION, *by Joseph W. Garbarino, reprinted from* INDUSTRIAL RELATIONS, *vol. 10, no. 1, February 1971.*

. . . AND WHAT PROFESSORS THINK: ABOUT STUDENT PROTEST AND MANNERS, MORALS, POLITICS, AND CHAOS ON THE CAMPUS, *by Seymour Martin Lipset and Everett C. Ladd, Jr., reprinted from* PSYCHOLOGY TODAY, *November 1970.**

DEMAND AND SUPPLY IN U.S. HIGHER EDUCATION: A PROGRESS REPORT, *by Roy Radner and Leonard S. Miller, reprinted from* AMERICAN ECONOMIC REVIEW, *May 1970.**

RESOURCES FOR HIGHER EDUCATION: AN ECONOMIST'S VIEW, *by Theodore W. Schultz, reprinted from* JOURNAL OF POLITICAL ECONOMY, *vol. 76, no. 3, University of Chicago, May/ June 1968.**

INDUSTRIAL RELATIONS AND UNIVERSITY RELATIONS, *by Clark Kerr, reprinted from* PROCEEDINGS OF THE 21ST ANNUAL WINTER MEETING OF THE INDUSTRIAL RELATIONS RESEARCH ASSOCIATION, *pp. 15–25.**

NEW CHALLENGES TO THE COLLEGE AND UNIVERSITY, *by Clark Kerr, reprinted from Kermit Gordon (ed.),* AGENDA FOR THE NATION, *The Brookings Institution, Washington, D.C., 1968. **

PRESIDENTIAL DISCONTENT, *by Clark Kerr, reprinted from David C. Nichols (ed.),* PERSPECTIVES ON CAMPUS TENSIONS: PAPERS PREPARED FOR THE SPECIAL COMMITTEE ON CAMPUS TENSIONS, *American Council on Education, Washington, D.C., September 1970.**

STUDENT PROTEST—AN INSTITUTIONAL AND NATIONAL PROFILE, *by Harold Hodgkinson, reprinted from* THE RECORD, *vol. 71, no. 4, May 1970.**

WHAT'S BUGGING THE STUDENTS?, *by Kenneth Keniston, reprinted from* EDUCATIONAL RECORD, *American Council on Education, Washington, D.C., Spring 1970.**

THE POLITICS OF ACADEMIA, *by Seymour Martin Lipset, reprinted from David C. Nichols (ed.),* PERSPECTIVES ON CAMPUS TENSIONS: PAPERS PREPARED FOR THE SPECIAL COMMITTEE ON CAMPUS TENSIONS, *American Council on Education, Washington, D.C., September 1970.**

INTERNATIONAL PROGRAMS OF U.S. COLLEGES AND UNIVERSITIES: PRIORITIES FOR THE SEVENTIES, *by James A. Perkins, reprinted by permission of the International Council for Educational Development, Occasional Paper no. 1, July 1971.*

FACULTY UNIONISM: FROM THEORY TO PRACTICE, *by Joseph W. Garbarino, reprinted from* INDUSTRIAL RELATIONS, *vol. 11, no. 1, pp. 1–17, February 1972.*

*The Commission's stock of this reprint has been exhausted.